ALTERNATIVE FUTURES FOR WORSHIP

Reconciliation

ALTERNATIVE FUTURES
FOR WORSHIP

Volume 4
Reconciliation

Volume Editor

PETER E. FINK, S.J.

Authors

PAUL J. ROY, S.J.
DENIS J. WOODS
PETER E. FINK, S.J.
WALTER H. CUENIN

THE LITURGICAL PRESS
Collegeville, Minnesota 56321

Cover design by Mary Jo Pauly

Manufactured in the United States of America.

ISBN 0-8146-1496-5

1   2   3   4   5   6   7   8

Library of Congress Cataloging-in-Publication Data
Alternative futures for worship.

Includes bibliographies.
Contents: v. 1. General Introduction / volume editor, Regis A. Duffy ; authors, Michael A. Cowan, Paul J. Philibert, Edward J. Kilmartin — v. 2. Baptism and confirmation / edited by Mark Searle ; by Andrew D. Thompson . . . [et al.] — v. 3. The eucharist / edited by Bernard J. Lee ; by Thomas Richstatter . . . [et al.] — [etc.]
1. Sacraments (Liturgy) 2. Catholic Church—Liturgy. I. Lee, Bernard J., 1932–
BX2200.A49   1987   265   86-27300
ISBN 0-8146-1491-4 (set)

CONTENTS

The Contributors   7

Preface
    Bernard J. Lee, S.M.   11

Introduction
    Peter E. Fink, S.J.   13

1. Psychological Dimensions of Reconciliation
    Paul J. Roy, S.J.   17

2. Reconciliation of Groups
    Denis J. Woods   33

3. Reconciliation and Forgiveness:
   A Theological Reflection
    Peter E. Fink, S.J.   43

4. History of the Sacrament of Reconciliation
    Peter E. Fink, S.J.   73

RITUALS

Alternative 1:
Communal Celebration of the Sacrament of Reconciliation
with Individual Presentation of Sins and Individual Absolution
    Walter H. Cuenin   93

Alternative 2:
Liturgy of Reconciliation Where Unordained Ministers Receive

the Confession of Sin, Pray for Forgiveness and Reconciliation,
and Together Present This for Confirmation and Completion
in the Liturgical Assembly
   Peter E. Fink, S.J.   109

Alternative 3:
Liturgy for a Christian Day of Atonement
   Peter E. Fink, S.J.   127

Alternative 4:
Liturgy for the Reconciliation of Groups
   Peter E. Fink, S.J., and Denis J. Woods   147

Index   167

THE CONTRIBUTORS

PETER E. FINK, S.J., is associate professor of liturgical theology at the Weston School of Theology and has been a frequent contributor to *Worship* and other professional journals.

PAUL J. ROY, S.J., is assistant professor of pastoral counseling at the Weston School of Theology and a psychotherapist in private practice in Cambridge, Massachusetts.

DENIS J. WOODS taught social ethics at the Weston School of Theology from 1983 to 1985. He is the director of the Housing Assistance Center in Buffalo, New York.

WALTER H. CUENIN is associate pastor of Sacred Heart Church in Lexington, Massachusetts, and adjunct associate professor of sacraments and liturgy at the Weston School of Theology.

ALTERNATIVE FUTURES FOR WORSHIP
Reconciliation

PREFACE

Alternative Futures for Worship is not a product. It is rather a window through which a relationship may be observed. Or to change the image, it is a listening device with which a conversation may be overheard. The participants are sacramental theology, liturgical experience, and the human sciences.

All of life—like all the world—has the possibility of mediating the transformative encounter between God and human history. That is its sacramental character. In the Roman Catholic tradition there has evolved over a long history a system of seven sacraments. These are not our only sacramental experiences. But they occupy a privileged sacramental role in the life of this Christian community.

Each sacrament concerns itself with the religious meanings of some important slice of human life. There are not many slices of life whose patterns and interpreted meanings have not been probed and described by the human sciences. It is crucial, therefore, that sacramental and liturgical theology pay very careful attention indeed to the deliverances of the human sciences. Religious experience cannot, of course, be reduced to the descriptive reports of the human sciences. Yet it would be foolhardy to theologize or "liturgize" apart from serious consideration of these many empirical attempts to understand the character of lived experience in our culture and our time.

Each volume in this series exemplifies the processes of encounter between sacrament, liturgy, and the human sciences: what reports from the human sciences are being considered; how do these understandings affect the meaning structure of the sacrament; how would these meanings find liturgical expression. Every volume in the series has this fundamental agenda, but each takes it up in its own particular way. Our aims are modest; we have not intended to produce any exactly right conclusion. We only care to engage in serious, imaginative, and highly responsible conversation.

It may seem that proposing alternative sacramental rituals is irresponsible, and it would be if they were proposed for anyone's actual use. They are not! This is not an underground sacramentary. We are most aware of the tentative and groping character of each of these attempts.

However, we believe with William James that the best way to understand what something means (like this conversation between Christian experience and the human sciences) is to see what difference it makes. James says you must set an idea to work in the stream of experience to know what it means. We choose ritual as that stream of experience.

Sacramental rituals are not themselves the sacraments. The sacraments are temporally thick slices of life which through time mediate religious experience. The liturgical rite is but one moment in this thicker-than-rite sacramentalization of life. It is a privileged moment though. Ritual is a moment of high value if it illuminates and intensifies the meaning of sacrament. Leonard Bernstein's "Mass for Theatre" speaks movingly of the absurdity of ritual when it has lost touch with the lives of the people who are supposed to be celebrating it. When private meanings and public ritual meanings do not intersect (which is not to say coincide), the absurdity is thundering.

Because a ritual puts a sacramental understanding under the spotlight, we have elected to explore the conversation between sacramental life and the human sciences by imagining ritual appropriations of the fruits of the conversation. That is our way of setting an idea to work imaginatively in the stream of experience. That, and nothing more! But that is a lot.

We suggest that any readers of this volume who have not done so read the introductory volume. There we have tried to say more fully what we think we are about in this entire series and why the many authors who contributed to it are convinced that this project is a quite right thing to do. We are happy to have you listen in on our conversation. Our long-term hope is that you may join it.

Bernard J. Lee, S.M.
San Antonio, Texas

INTRODUCTION

Peter E. Fink, S.J.

> All this is from God, who through Christ reconciled us to himself
> and gave us the ministry of reconciliation; that is, in Christ God
> was reconciling the world to himself, not counting their trespasses
> against them, and entrusting to us the message of reconciliation
> (2 Cor 5:18-19).

The sacrament of reconciliation and forgiveness is that activity
of the Church, set in motion in obedience to the Word of God and
in the power of the Holy Spirit, which seeks to respond to the reality of sin with the healing grace of Jesus Christ. The primary sacrament of reconciliation after Christ himself is, of course, the Church
in all the ways it seeks to counter the forces of sin in the world.
The liturgical enactment of this sacrament is, like all sacraments,
"the outstanding means by which the faithful can express in their
lives, and manifest to others, the mystery of Christ and the real
nature of the true church" (Constitution on the Sacred Liturgy, 2).
This liturgical action is envisioned as reconciliation where sin is seen
to rupture relationship. It is enacted as penance where sin demands
some absolution of debt. It is called humble confession where sin
is a hardness of heart which demands open and sincere acknowledgement of the truth of one's actions before God and before others.
Its names and its contours vary with the understanding of the ways
of sin, but always its goal and its purpose is the same: to undo,
heal, and transform sin and its destructive effect. "But that you may
know that the Son of Man has authority on earth to forgive sins,
I say to you, rise, take up your pallet, and go home" (Mark 2:10-11).

In the years since the Second Vatican Council, this sacramental activity of the Church has entered a new phase. Liturgical history has commonly distinguished between *canonical* penance and *private* penance, to name the two major periods in the history of the sacrament from the beginning to the present. The first evolved around an understanding of sin as disruption in the communal life of the Church, which demanded public reconciliation with God and with the Church. The second developed from a model of sin as some form of "code violation" and sought to insure absolution from the debt incurred. Both, of course, involved some form of renovation and reformation of life.

At the beginning of this new third phase, where the understanding of sin is again in evolution, and where the need for the Gospel healing of Christ is coming to surface in a variety of new ways, one thing is clear. Contemporary awareness of sin does not allow itself to be neatly packaged. Though surely it includes both a rupture in relationship and a violation of God's law, it involves something larger and deeper as well. The reality of sin is elusive to name, yet nonetheless keenly felt. It seeks, as it has in the past, new arenas in which it can be overcome by the grace and action of Jesus Christ.

In light of the many faces with which sin shows itself in contemporary experience, ranging from the intensely personal sin that torments individuals to the global sin that inflicts oppression and injustice, the future of this ecclesial activity will certainly not be content with a single mode of expression. The chapters presented in this volume are an attempt to set a context for the future that may evolve. The rituals presented as alternatives attempt to give concrete shape to at least some imaginings of this future. In the end, of course, only the living Church can shape and embrace what that future will be.

The Church's mission remains the mission of Christ: to stamp out the evil of sin and to establish upon the earth the healing ministry of reconciliation. The Church's task is to develop liturgical and other forms of action that are appropriate to that mission. The hope of this volume is to contribute a small piece to the fulfillment of that task.

The lead chapters by Paul Roy and Denis Woods raise issues from the social sciences which challenge both the theology and the *praxis* of sacramental reconciliation in our day. Roy speaks to the question of reconciliation within individual persons and in the interpersonal arena between individuals. He looks at the psychological processes involved in such reconciliation and challenges liturgical theology to take those processes seriously. Woods raises a challenge of a different sort. His expertise and experience has been with groups rather than individuals, and he notes the almost total lack of concern in the tradition of sacramental reconciliation with the task of reconciling groups. Yet most of the divisions and conflicts that exist in today's world, he observes, are among groups. In the task of imagining the future of this sacrament, Woods' challenge is particularly poignant.

My own theological and historical chapters enter into dialogue with the presentations of both Roy and Woods. In the theological piece I explore first the levels of division that need reconciliation, levels that span the psychological, the institutional, and the moral dimensions of human life. I then examine Jesus' own human journey, both to understand the path to reconciliation and to illuminate the nature and role of the sacrament which invites others into the journey of Jesus himself. A final section in this theological chapter seeks to understand the ways of conversion, specifically God's role, our role, and the workings of the two together.

The historical chapter is more a reflection on the historical shapes this sacrament has taken than on the specific details of the shapes themselves. This chapter is governed by two perspectives: the chapters that precede it from the human sciences and from liturgical theology, on the one hand, and the alternative future rituals which this volume presents, on the other.

Ritual I by Walter Cuenin is offered as a mild evolution from the current official ritual offerings and is named a future "already-in-the-making," rather than a future which is far off. Its purpose is to serve as the ordinary context in which the truth of reconciliation and God's forgiveness in Christ is regularly rehearsed in the prayer-faith life of the local Church. Ritual II by myself grows out of three concerns: first, a need which surfaces in Paul Roy's chapter for a plurality of ministers, men and women, for this sacrament; second, a phenomenon already in motion whereby ordained priests and nonordained religious and lay persons are asked to serve as "reconcilers" in a variety of contexts, especially in hospital chaplaincy, retreat direction, and spiritual direction; and third, a suggestion which surfaces in Cuenin's piece concerning the possible shortage of ordained presbyters to serve the reconciling ministry. Ritual III, also by myself, brings a praying community into consciousness of the larger reality of sin and evil over which mere human power alone is useless. Sin in community, in the Church, and in the world seeks to be addressed by the Gospel of Christ, and in the tradition of the Jewish Day of Atonement is placed trustingly into God's healing hands. The final ritual by Denis Woods and myself together is an attempt to stretch the sacramental tradition firmly into the arena of group reconciliation.

These rituals, as I say, are some ways of imagining the future. There are others. Two which are not included in this volume deserve at least to be mentioned for the purpose of expanding even further the imagination of the reader. One, developed by Fr. Robert Blondell of the archdiocese of Detroit and presented by Cardinal Joseph Bernardin to the Synod of Bishops, patterns reconciliation after the Rite of Christian Initiation of Adults. An order of penitents parallels the order of catechumens. This is itself an ancient ritual pattern that is important to recapture. The second, developed more informally by Sr. Mary Collins, O.S.B., until recently of the faculty of The Catholic University, employs the model of the parish mission. Her concept is a week long "Festival of Reconciliation," with a variety of activities to urge and bring about reconciliation in a community. Both of these were invited to participate in this project but were unfortunately unable to do so.

It is a time for imagining. The Second Vatican Council served to open up the past by restoring to contemporary faith and prayer richness of the past that had disappeared from view. And by opening the past it likewise opened the future. If the work of this volume, and indeed the work of this whole series, serves to put concrete shape on the ways we imagine the future, it will serve its purpose well. May the people be served, and may the reconciling mission which the Church has received from Christ carry on.

Peter E. Fink, S.J.
Weston School of Theology
Cambridge, Massachusetts

1. PSYCHOLOGICAL DIMENSIONS OF RECONCILIATION

Paul J. Roy, S.J.

Introduction

The story of Adam and Eve as recorded in Genesis can be reflected upon and understood from a variety of viewpoints. It is a literary piece and can be examined from the perspective of literary style and structure. It is a biblical piece and can fall under the watchful eye of the biblical exegete and the form critic. It is certainly a theological piece and can therefore feed the musings and meanderings of theological reflection. And it is a piece about human life and is therefore attractive for study to the whole range of the human sciences.

In this chapter I propose to view the story through the lens of human psychology. From the psychological perspective the story of Adam and Eve is a myth about human beings involved in the struggle of growing up. It addresses psychological tasks that must be recognized and completed, or at least consciously worked at, simply because we are human. These tasks are summed up in the idea that *we must grow up*, that is, that we must become *individuals* while at the same time being *connected to others*.

By virtue of our humanity, we stand in relationship to all else that is, and so we must learn to be independent, autonomous, and interdependent all at the same time. When these three are not real and harmonious in our lives, we experience division and separation, conflict and violence. It is at this point psychologically that we stand in need of reconciliation.

The way in which we can be reconciled within ourselves and within the community of human beings that makes up our world is a function both of the ways in which the human psyche comes to an awareness of itself and of the ways in which the world affects and shapes that awareness. In the pages that follow I will look at some of the psychological and cultural elements that make the process of reconciliation within an individual and between persons both necessary and possible.

Cultural Forces That Foster Division

One factor that must be taken into account in any reflection on reconciliation and division is the influence which a given culture exerts on its people. It is in the spirit of the Western world to divide. At least a good portion of our experience of the world, of life, and of interaction with others, is the experience of division and separation. It has become an important value in American culture to be able to stand apart as an individual, singled out and therefore separated because of status, prestige, wealth, talent, accomplishment, intellect, or power.

As men and women grow up in this culture, they quickly learn the "rugged individualism" that is a part of their national heritage. They are encouraged to self-sufficiency. They are discouraged from being beholden to anyone. While some degree of conformity is often required in order to belong, it is uniqueness, not conformity, that is more often prized. That uniqueness is all the more valued when it places one closer to being "number one."

Certainly American national policies hold as ideals being the strongest, the wealthiest, the most powerful, and the most dominant force in the world. In another arena Americans strive to stand alone on the Olympian pedestal as winners of the gold. Our sports teams vie for World Series and Super Bowl victories that let them lay claim to "world" championships, even when no other country has competed. Television programs idealize the individual who fights evil and who fights the system, the "Lone Ranger of the Old West" or the unmarried, unconnected cop or private eye of the contemporary scene.

At the same time that individualism is idealized and seen as heroic, the place of separation in our lives is trivialized. Divorce, for example, is treated as commonplace, with little attention being paid to the damage it brings to the lives of a great number of people.

Using people is glamorized on the "Soaps." Violence is the normal fare on television and in the movies, and also in music and novels. All this tends to numb people to the sacredness of human life, the holiness of human love, and the importance of the process of dying.

Conflict is more readily dealt with by a flex of national muscle rather than by negotiation. Disagreement is countered with weapons, vigilantes, invasions, and threats.

Even in our schools, in our churches, and in our places of work, the spirit of competition prevails over the spirit of cooperation. More often than not it is the progress of one person that serves as a measure for the progress of others, and that determines what is success and what is not. The philosophy of divide and conquer, insofar as it is applied in all these areas of life, is all too effective in pitting one person against another. The net result is that people end up feeling separate, divided from one another, and defeated.

Growing up and surviving in our culture have often posed the questions of how much power can be amassed and how much control can be wrested for one's own individual ends. Growing up and surviving have often meant acquiring domination over others, achieving superiority, and getting the upper hand. In a culture so replete with pressures for division and separation, the value of reconciliation seems small, and the task of reconciliation large indeed.

There are, however, signs of a "counter voice" in our culture that wants to challenge this individualistic way of relating to others. There are other values, other movements of the human spirit, other possibilities for new directions, and new ways of both growing up and surviving. The contemporary women's movement and the peace movement are but two examples that present alternative ways of relating to other human beings and indeed of relating to ourselves. People in these movements seem to have recognized the inhumanity of our ways and the ineffectiveness of human relationships based on criteria of superiority and inferiority. They have recognized the death-dealing aspect of division and separation. They are a hopeful voice for reconciliation in a culture that is intent on dividing.

The culture of any people is a strong determining factor in the task of reconciliation among and within individuals. It has to be said from the beginning that the specific culture in which this volume is being written exerts a strong negative influence on the task. It must also be recognized, however, that this same culture does contain some positive rays that brighten the task.

Psychological Challenges Toward Reconciliation

The tenor of our culture, and indeed of the world in the 1980's, seems to be such that becoming an individual is made, at one and the same time, both necessary and all but impossible. Some will argue that this has been true in every age of human history. If such is the case, then it may well be that we human beings are forever reluctant to take this life task upon ourselves. It seems to me, however, that the human race, and in particular the people of our day, deserve to be credited with a more optimistic appraisal.

Under the sign of optimism, and because the aim of this work is indeed to foster the possibility of reconciliation, I would like to explore three psychological theories which engage various aspects of the process of growing up and becoming an individual. My hope is to shed some light on the need for and the possibility of reconciliation within ourselves and among ourselves. The three are derived from Carl Jung, Erik Erikson, and Lillian Rubin.

CARL JUNG

Carl Jung wrote that "the sole and natural carrier of life is the individual."[1] At the center of Jungian psychology is the process of becoming an individual. Jung saw the Self to be "the central source of life energy, the fountain of our being which is most simply described as God."[2] Thus the Self is the seat of objective identity, the center of psychic being that takes in both the conscious and the unconscious. In addition there is a second center of psychic being which Jung called ego.

Since there are these two autonomous centers of psychic being, the relation between the two centers is seen to be of vital importance. According to one Jungian scholar, E. F. Edinger, "many of the vicissitudes of psychological development can be understood in terms of the changing relation between ego and Self at various stages of psychic growth."[3]

At the beginning of life, ego and Self are identified with each other and the unconscious. Thus there is actually no ego. As a person becomes more conscious, he or she is involved in a process whereby the ego gradually separates itself from the Self, while at the same time remaining connected to the Self. Edinger suggests that throughout life we are involved in a process of ego-Self separation and ego-Self union.

Jung defined individuation as "the development of the psychological individual as a differentiated being from the general, collective psychology. Individuation, therefore, is a *process of differentiation*, having for its goal the development of the individual personality."[4]

In another work Jung wrote: "The Self, like the unconscious, is an *a priori* existent out of which the ego evolves. It is, so to speak, an unconscious prefiguration of the ego."[5]

What is involved in individuation, therefore, is the struggle of the ego to become aware of (conscious of) itself in such a way that its uniqueness and individuality are recognized, its connectedness to all other individuals is acknowledged, and its link to the Self is maintained in integrity.

Jung and his followers have realized that this process of becoming an individual is one that necessarily puts the person (ego) in conflict or tension with God (the Self). Edinger has likened the process to the conflict which is expressed in the Adam and Eve myth and which gives us our theological concept of original sin: "Eating the forbidden fruit marks the transition from the eternal state of unconscious oneness with the self (the mindless, animal state) to a real, conscious life in space and time. In short, the myth symbolizes the birth of this ego. The effect of this birth process is to alienate the ego from its origins."[6]

The myth of the fall of humanity, suggests Edinger, is one that expresses a pattern or process that we go through in some way each time we arrive at greater consciousness. Thus the action of Adam and Eve, while it has been described as shameful, could also be seen as heroic, because they have sacrificed "the passive comfort of obedience for greater consciousness."[7]

The human experience of choosing consciousness over comfort, of moving outside of the Self, is one that forces us to live with the tension of shame and heroism. The more we choose to be conscious, the more we will sense the paradox that we are *both* separated *and* connected, and responsible to each of these aspects of our being at the same time. We feel separated from all that is and therefore feel estranged. Yet at the same time we know something of our uniqueness.

Edinger compares the experience of being an individual to that of being an only child, an experience which has both a positive and a negative aspect: "The positive aspect is the experience of being the favored one, of having no rivals with whom to compete for the available attention, interest, and love. The negative aspect of being an only child is that it means being lonely."[8]

The struggle and the challenge, then, is to transform the loneliness into aloneness and in that aloneness to accept the fact of being favored as a unique individual. It is to come to a conviction that we have a right to exist as we actually are, neither superior nor inferior to anyone else. This conviction, if firmly planted, eliminates the need to be defensive about ourselves or competitive with others. It refuses to identify our individuality with any particular talent, function, or aspect of ourselves. "The theological equivalent to this experience is justification before God."[9]

This brief sketch of pertinent aspects of Jungian psychology presents a first example of the psychological need for and possibility of reconciliation. Growing in consciousness and in awareness of our individuality will put us in conflict with ourselves, with our God, and with the people around us. If we do not surrender consciously to the power of the unconscious, that is, if we do not bring the process of individuation into reality, then we risk doing violence to our relationships and to our very selves. We therefore stand in need of reconciliation. It is possible to avoid this violence, however, and find reconciliation if on our own resources or with the help of others, we allow the process of individuation to unfold in its own proper way.

ERIK H. ERIKSON

Erikson described eight stages of development, each with its crisis and its specific challenges. Emerging from the eight critical periods of development are ego qualities, "criteria by which the individual demonstrates that his (or her) ego, at a given stage, is strong enough to integrate the timetable of the organism with the structure of social institutions."[10]

For Erikson consideration of the environment and of the network of social interactions was essential to the understanding of human development. It was not simply the ego's emergence into consciousness but also the context of the person's life that needed to be taken into account. The growth of the individual from birth through the development of identity to maturity and old age included a series of "choices" which determined how the individual would perceive the world and would function in that world.

The eight stages described by Erikson[11] along with their psychosocial conflicts are given in the chart below:

Erikson's Eight Psychosocial Stages

Infancy	—Basic Trust vs. Basic Mistrust
Early Childhood	—Autonomy vs. Shame and Doubt
Play Age	—Initiative vs. Guilt
School Age	—Industry vs. Inferiority
Adolescence	—Identity vs. Identity Confusion
Young Adulthood	—Intimacy vs. Isolation
Adulthood	—Generativity vs. Stagnation
Mature Adulthood	—Integrity vs. Despair and Disgust

Explanations of these stages can be found in Erikson's *Childhood and Society* and in a number of commentaries by authors who have studied Erikson's work from different vantage points.[12]

Erikson was quick to insist, however, that charts are simply tools to think with, not prescriptions to abide by. "If the chart . . . lists a series of conflicts or crises, we do not consider all development a series of crises: we claim only that psychosocial development proceeds by critical steps—'critical' being a characteristic of turning points, of moments of decision between progress and regression, integration and retardation."[13]

Erikson argued that the way we looked at the world was largely a function of the posture from which we perceived the world. New postures, therefore, lead to new perspectives, and new perspectives lead to new ways of actively engaging the world. The term Erikson used for these ways of engaging the world is "psychosocial modalities," and he described modalities that correspond to each stage of development.

Thus the first social modality learned in life is that of *getting*, that is, of receiving and accepting what is given. Erikson adds: "One may say (somewhat mystically, to be sure) that in thus *getting what is given*, and in learning to *get somebody to do* for him what he wishes to have done, the baby also develops the necessary ego groundwork to *get to be* a giver."[14] So the infant in this stage *learns* to "get" and to "give in return."

The mutuality and reciprocity of these modalities, which point to *interaction* with the world, continue in each successive stage. In the second stage the child learns to "hold on" and to "let go." The child at the third stage must learn the modality of "making," that is, of going after, "in the sense of 'being on the make.' "[15] Learning to "make things," to "be somebody," to "be with others," to "take care of others," and "to be, through having been" characterize stages four to eight respectively.

In all of this, environment is crucial. As Donald Capps points out, "this whole developmental plan can be hampered or thwarted by an inhospitable environment. A harmful social environment may inhibit or arrest growth in any given stage."[16]

The ideal implied in Erikson's theory is that the individual should move through each of the psychological conflicts and thereby develop the ego qualities that are exemplified in the "positive" side of the conflict. Therefore the ideals are trust, autonomy, initiative, industry, identity, intimacy, generativity, and integrity.

The theory also asserts that autonomy is achieved only if there is basic trust, that initiative is possible only through autonomy, and so forth. In other words the ego qualities build upon one another in successive stages.

Since trust, autonomy, and initiative are foundational in this theory, let me examine these first three developmental stages for what insights they might shed on the human process of growing up and the simultaneous need for reconciliation, both within an individual and between persons.

The first of the basic conflicts of life involves the question of whether or not we live in a world and with people who are dependable. For the infant basic trust implies that he or she has "learned to rely on the sameness and continuity of the outer providers,"[17] as well as to consider himself or herself trustworthy. This, writes Erikson, forms the basis of the child's future sense of identity, which identity will be a combination of a "sense of being 'all right', of being oneself, and of becoming what other people trust one will become."[18]

What is important for our discussion here is Erikson's observation that even under the best of circumstances, this first stage of development brings to the psychic life a "sense of inner division and universal nostalgia for a paradise forfeited."[19] This comes to the infant through parental prohibitions and permissions, and it is against this experience of deprivation, division, and abandonment that basic trust must maintain itself throughout life.

The second developmental conflict involves the question of control. Physical and muscular maturation lead to exploration of two social modalities, holding on and letting go. Says Erikson: "to hold can become a destructive and cruel retaining, and it can become a pattern of care: to have and to hold. To let go, too, can turn into an inimical letting loose of destructive forces, or it can become a relaxed 'to let pass' and 'to let be.' "[20]

The denial of the experience of the autonomy of free choice will lead a child to seek to gain power and control over the environment through manipulation of self and others. "This stage, therefore, becomes decisive for the ratio of love and hate, cooperation and willfulness, freedom of self-expression and its suppression. From a sense of self-control without loss of self-esteem comes a lasting sense of good will and pride; from a sense of loss of self-control and of foreign overcontrol comes a lasting propensity for doubt and shame."[21]

Here again there is potential for wholeness and cooperation, or for division within and among individuals. The human need for reconciliation can arise if this second developmental crisis is poorly met or incompletely resolved.

In the third developmental stage Erikson describes the crisis as unfolding in the aggressiveness that follows the acquisition of a sense of autonomy. Initiative is the positive and desirable side of this crisis. Its introduction adds to autonomy the quality of "undertaking, planning and 'attacking' a task for the sake of being active and on the move . . ."[22]

The danger, which is the negative side of this crisis, lies in the sense of guilt that can come when one's initiative moves beyond the individual's capacity and becomes aggressive manipulation and coercion. While in the previous stage the danger was that autonomy could lead to jealousy, in this stage initiative can lead to rivalry with others who are potentially more powerful or more capable. Failure in the rivalry usually results in resignation, guilt, and anxiety. "Here the most fateful split and transformation in the emotional powerhouse occurs, a split between potential human glory and potential total destruction."[23]

It is at this stage that conscience begins to be developed, that children experience hate for parents who have something to do with the formation of conscience, and that individuals sometimes seek to stave off their guilt through self-righteousness and the inhibition of that very initiative that can be so creative, exciting, and life-giving.

These observations from Erikson point to yet other sources of conflict and division that threaten the human process of growing up, and they suggest both the need for and the task of reconciliation in that process. Reconciliation is needed if the individual is to retain and develop a sense of initiative that is unparalyzed by guilt and that can lead to proper identity formation and ultimately to integrity of life. Proper guidance through the various developmental stages will in effect be this reconciliation.

LILLIAN B. RUBIN

A final psychological theory I would like to look at is found in the work of Lillian Rubin in her important book, *Intimate Strangers.* This work, too, can help us understand what it is that brings human beings to the need for reconciliation. It can therefore help us see the various elements of the reconciliation process itself. The book is subtitled, "Men and Women Together," and it looks at how characteristics of the male and female personalities emerge in individuals and what these have to do with the way individuals relate to each other.

Boys and girls have very different tasks in developing gender identity, and Rubin insists that these tasks, as well as the psychological differences that stem from them, are a response to the social situation into which children are born more than they are inherent in the nature of human development.

I pay attention to Rubin's work here, because she deals with interpersonal relationships and intimacy in those relationships, with a view to understanding the psychological differences between women and men. If it is true—and I believe it is—that many of the conflicts experienced in our age, from sibling rivalry to marital problems to war between nations, come from the ease with which human beings claim superiority over one another, and if it is also true—and I believe it is—that the paradigmatic experience of that sense of superiority is found in the ways in which men have insisted they are superior to women, then it is of crucial importance for us to consider how the process may be reversed. It is important for all of us, men and women alike, to come to an understanding of the source of the conflict and to reconcile our deepest desires for life and for peace with that in our social structures which can fulfill or thwart those desires.

The premise for Rubin's theory is the fact that in our society it is almost always a woman who is the primary caregiver of infancy: *"And no fact of our early life has greater consequences for how girls and boys develop into women and men, therefore for how we relate to each other in our adult years."*[24]

The primary caregiver of our infant lives is the person to whom we make our first attachment and the one with whom we first identify. So whether you are male or female, your most primitive experience of both attachment and identification is with a woman. When infancy passes the task of the child is one of separation and individuation. The child must find independence and identity apart from the primary caregiver, indeed apart from all others who have entered his or her social milieu.

Separation and unity become the dominant themes of this period of life, and the child "lives in ambivalent oscillation between the desire first for one, then for the other."[25] These will remain continuing themes in adult life as well.

The separation process is a complicated one, and it requires both the crystallization of gender identity and the maintenance of the personal psychological boundaries of the self that differentiate each of us and set us off from the rest of the world. The struggle to meet these two requirements is different for boys than it is for girls, precisely because it is a woman who has mothered them both.

Put in its most simple terms, the task for the boy who has been raised by a woman is to identify with his maleness by renouncing his connection with the first person outside of his own self to have been internalized into his psychic world. The conflict and the pain come from the fact that "identification and attachment are so closely linked that the child cannot give up one without assault on the other. With the repression of the identification with mother, therefore, the attachment to her becomes ambivalent."[26] It is at this point that the male child builds a set of defenses, a protection against the pain brought about from this radical shift in his world, that will remain a part of him in his adult life. "This is the beginning of the development of ego boundaries that are fixed and firm—barriers that rigidly separate self from other, that circumscribe not only his relationships with others but his connection to his inner emotional life as well."[27]

The process is quite different for girls and carries with it an entirely different set of obstacles. In the normal course of development, a girl's formation of gender identity does not require the kind of breaks with the past that were part of the boy's individuation and separation. Consequently the girl does not experience the need to build defenses against feeling and attachment. The struggle here involves the problem of separating. What is more difficult for girls is to define and experience the self as an autonomous, bounded individual.

Thus the parameters within which we struggle to relate to each other are those of separation and unity. "For women, the issue of maintaining separation dominates; for men, it's sustaining unity that is so difficult—problems that make themselves felt around every important issue in a marriage, from the conflicts we experience around intimacy and dependency to the way we parent our children."[28]

These psychological differences between men and women have their roots in the interaction between individuals and society. In its broadest terms what has happened is that society has divided rationality and emotionality among men and women and in the process has created a rift between men and women that must be reconciled. In fact, "thought, defined as the ultimate good, has been assigned to men; feeling, considered at best a problem, has fallen to women."[29] Rubin goes on to say that "intuitively, women try to heal the split that these definitions of male and female have foisted on us."[30]

Rubin's work is important for any consideration of the process of reconciliation, because she brings to the surface divisive factors that all too frequently escape notice. The ways in which we define ourselves and others must be taken into account, and where such definitions are indeed a source of conflict and division, they must be challenged and revised. In addition the effect that our social structures and institutions have on the ways we grow up and try to survive in this world need to be examined and constantly evaluated. Where they produce division and conflict, they must be challenged and changed, or else ways must be found for people to avoid their harmful effects.

Concluding Remarks

Jung, Erikson, and Rubin, each in a unique way, suggest that becoming an individual in our society is inevitably bound up in conflict. Whether it is the rebellion from the Self, or the acquiring of autonomy and the exercise of initiative, or the separation from parents, growing up involves us in some way in the myth of Adam and Eve, in a move from innocence to the loss of innocence, in a struggle to be self-determining, in the tension between separation and unity. From them we can come to understand some of the elements that must go into the process of reconciliation, both within the individual and between persons.

From Jung we get the notion of the ego's rebellion from the Self. The rebellion is in essence a willingness to accept one's own individuality without becoming individualistic.[31] It is to acknowledge that each of us is an "only child," and therefore favored, while at the same time accepting our connectedness to everything that is.

From Erikson we get the importance of establishing basic trust in the world, of becoming autonomous, and of exercising initiative. We must do this even in the face of a world that often seems untrustworthy, even at the risk of personal shame and even if it means moving beyond the fear of appearing to be inferior.

Finally from Rubin we gain an understanding of the importance of gender identity and of the enormous influence our early attachments exercise on the ways we relate to one another. Our culture has set up ideals for men and women that become sources of division, misunderstanding, and conflict, not only in relationships between men and women but ultimately even in relations between groups, races, and nations. The differences pointed to by Rubin suggest that the ways in which we establish boundaries for ourselves, whether to achieve separation or to maintain independence, can become important factors in our search for reconciliation in all our relationships.

I distinguished at the beginning of the chapter between a theological and a psychological reading of the Adam and Eve myth. From a psychological vantage point this myth and the process of reconciliation itself do not have anything to do with sin. Psychological existence is separate from sin as the theologian may define it. Nonetheless even on the psychological plane people do experience division in their lives and even on the psychological plane need to be reconciled. Theologian and psychologist identify the same basic human need.

I would suggest, then, that when we enter the realm of faith and move to examine the ways in which sin does indeed enter human lives, the basic elements of human development which have been articulated by people like Jung, Erikson, and Rubin must be taken into serious account. In order to bring ourselves to reconciliation, we must pay attention to the psychology of the process. This will entail, first of all, an acknowledgement and an appreciation of the individuality and the uniqueness of each human person. Each as a child of God, is favored in herself or himself and is by that fact connected to every other child of God.

In addition the reconciliation process requires the establishment of basic trust, a confidence in the trustworthiness of the world or at least some parts of the world. It requires also encouragement to and support of the individual as an autonomous person who can take initiative in living his or her life.

Finally it is crucial that the attitudes which we derive from our culture and from social structures that control our lives be examined and "converted." Specifically our needs for separation and unity, which we learn to meet often at the expense of healthy relationships, must be put in a new light, so that a spirit of domination and subservience will not be allowed to govern our ways of relating to others.

In the end what we seek through reconciliation is in reality the fullest and healthiest expression of our humanity. For it is as human beings that we grow up, realize our individuality, and join with others in bringing creation to its completion.

Footnotes

1. C. G. Jung, *The Practice of Psychotherapy*, Collected Works (CW) vol. 16, 1954, par. 224.
2. E. F. Edinger, *Ego and Archetype* (New York: Penguin Books, 1972) 4.
3. *Ibid.*
4. Jung, *Psychological Types*, CW, vol. 6, par. 755.
5. Jung, *Psychology and Religion: West and East*, CW, vol. 11, 1958, par. 139.
6. Edinger, *Ego and Archetype* 18.
7. *Ibid.* 21.
8. *Ibid.* 178.
9. *Ibid.* 167.
10. E. H. Erikson, *Childhood and Society*, 2nd ed. (New York: Norton, 1963) 246.
11. *Ibid.* 247–274.
12. See, for example, Donald Capps, *Life Cycle Theory and Pastoral Care*; Robert Coles, *Erik H. Erikson: The Growth of His Work* (Philadelphia: Fortress, 1983).
13. Erikson, *Childhood and Society* 270–271.
14. *Ibid.* 76.
15. *Ibid.* 90.
16. Capps, *Life Cycle Theory* 24.
17. Erikson, *Childhood and Society* 248.
18. *Ibid.* 249.
19. *Ibid.* 250.
20. *Ibid.* 251.
21. *Ibid.* 254.
22. *Ibid.* 255.

23. *Ibid.* 256.

24. Lillian B. Rubin, *Intimate Strangers* (New York: Harper and Row, 1983) 42–43.

25. *Ibid.* 51.

26. *Ibid.* 56.

27. *Ibid.*

28. *Ibid.* 64.

29. *Ibid.* 72.

30. *Ibid.* 73.

31. See Frieda Fordham, *An Introduction to Jung's Psychology* (New York: Penguin Books, 1953) 69–83.

2. RECONCILIATION OF GROUPS

Denis J. Woods

The question to be discussed in this chapter is whether or not the sacrament of reconciliation can have any relevance for the reconciliation of groups. The question arises because much or most of the evil evident in our world comes out of divisions between groups, rather than from divisions between individuals or between an individual and a group. The sacrament of reconciliation, on the other hand, has been chiefly concerned with individual confession, personal admission of guilt, and personal repentance. It has been enacted and experienced as the reconciliation of an individual to the Church community, with the latter personalized in the priest, who acts on behalf of the community, usually without its knowledge, to communicate forgiveness and the assurance of reconciliation to the penitent. The question must honestly be asked whether such a rite can be of any use in healing the divisions in Church and society that are caused by controversial issues such as abortion. It must also be asked whether the sacrament can be of any use in reconciling two families that no longer speak to each other.

Three Kinds of Group Divisions

It will be worthwhile to recognize that not all group divisions are the same and that chances for reconciliation vary with the kind of split that exists. Let me suggest that divisions between groups are of three kinds, with some overlap in reality of course.

DISTRIBUTIVE DIVISIONS

The first kind of division occurs as the result of competition for shares of a very large pie. Each competitor comes away with a share. Perhaps none gets all it wanted, and perhaps one gets more of what it wanted than the others. It may be argued that one group profits at the expense of the others, and no group is happy with the muddy result. It also may be argued that the results for each group fall within the general range of justice. To the political analyst this is the plus-sum game of distributive politics. There are divisions, but no real losers.

Collective bargaining about contracts between labor and management present the classic example of this kind of conflict. Occasionally the negotiations end with bad feelings and with a need for reconciliation. Similarly a tenants' group in public housing trying to deal with a municipal housing authority that is itself hard pressed for funds due to budget cuts, will come away with only a small portion of what was demanded but with a large dose of exasperation.

Such divisions may also result from arguments over less tangible goods or in the less public worlds of parish and family life. Groups dispute about procedures, priorities, and goals within a parish, and it is common enough for the families of a brother and sister to fall out for a while because of disagreement about roles in caring for a parent.

IDEOLOGICAL DIVISIONS

It is quite a different situation when the conflict is between two groups fighting over some value which cannot be divided up or when the groups insist for ideological reasons that the winner must take all. For example those who try to find a middle ground between the disputants in the abortion debate find themselves attacked from both sides. (See the issues of *Christianity and Crisis* for February 18 and March 31, 1980, for a case in point.) It is an ideological conflict in which many on both sides will not listen to what the other side has to say. The values admit no compromise, because they are perceived as literally involving life and death, both sides claiming with equal volume and certainty that they are choosing life while the others are angels of death.

Usually, as in the case of the abortion issue, the opponents do not know each other. The argument takes place across the length of the political spectrum, by means of statistics and the media, in Churches that have little contact with each other, and in the negative context of demonstrations and even violence. There is no common space for personal contact, much less for the binding of wounds or for reconciliation. It is a case of the Hatfields and the McCoys, tribal warfare with basic commitments to persons, groups and values, even if those values are not always well articulated, even if they are more assumed than examined. It is at base a commitment in faith.

Scaled down versions of the Hatfields and the McCoys are more common, as when the families of a brother and a sister go separate ways because of rivalry between two of their children. Commitment to the child regardless of the circumstances can produce a non-negotiable situation which threatens to explode while at the same time begging for reconciliation.

STRUCTURAL DIVISIONS

The third type represents the most serious division of all and the most difficult to reconcile. Here the winner does take all, because the world is structured in such a way that one group almost inevitably wins, and the other almost inevitably loses. The inevitability flows from the patterned action of a well-oiled machine, one that has sometimes been operating since farther back than anyone can remember. It can be as pervasive and destructive as the system of slavery or as positive as a paternalistic system, where generous shares are indeed allotted to all, but in ways that are determined by custom and not by choice.

In the paternalistic system there is no need for reconciliation until a group recognizes that it is deprived, or is about to be deprived, of an important value and has no choice in the matter. A bishop may close a parish or a school without consultation of the parishioners or parents, presenting a fait accompli and offering no recourse. The gatekeepers within the paternalistic structure will then refuse access to the one awesome person whom the parents or parishioners must reach. The structure determines that the decision maker will be the winner and will take all.

Residents of declining neighborhoods know something of the same exasperation. They see a gradual decline of maintenance, of services, of property values, and of cohesion. One day they realize that insecurity and fear have been growing in them for some time. But when they turn to find what it is that has caused their helpless state, they find no explanation except "market factors," a long line of invisible decisions by invisible people made over the course of a decade, inadvertently, anonymously, with no intent to harm, but with effects that finally become visible in shattered lives. Can the ground ever be recovered? Where does the fearful homeowner begin? In this case the exclusion has been from the system itself.

The same may be said of the many homeless who walk our streets with literally no place to go, of those poor who were stacked up in the worst examples of public housing, and of the many who find themselves towards life's end depressed and lost after a series of forced moves brought on by manipulated racial residential change. These examples also illustrate that the losers in an unjust structural situation are more likely to be atomized individuals rather than people who have something positive in common that binds them into a group.

The return of the Vietnam veterans exemplified this shattering experience. They found a divided, wounded country and themselves in a twilight zone of indifference and vague resentment. They had little in common beyond their tour of duty. They were deprived of any sense of whom they might be reconciled with. It is as if they were excluded from the argument and then blamed for being outside.

In such situations it is commonly the case that one group comes into the conflict with a disproportionate share of resources, and therefore of power, relative to the other. The fight is between the haves and the have-nots, who do not know each other face-to-face, but only across the long divides of residential patterns, or food delivery systems, or national and cultural boundaries. The resultant of forces in such a conflict will almost inevitably reinforce the division, and the outcome cannot easily be described as just.

So we have three kinds of groups in conflict and in need of reconciliation: first, the groups that compete in the pluralistic world with some share of power, but who stand apart from each other, at least in some areas of their lives; second, the groups that are in a winner-take-all fight with each other over real or perceived fundamental values; and third, the groups that are separated by an unjust social system, one group profiting from the system and the other excluded from it.

The Chance for Reconciliation

In the first type of group conflict, there is still a common ground on which the groups meet—across a bargaining table, in the parish hall, or in the many chambers of the political arena. In those spaces the groups continue to deal with each other, like poker players whose possibilities change from night to night—often from hand to hand—according to the cards, the stakes, the resources, the knowledge, the skill, and the stamina of the players. Everyone understands that there will be opposition, but no one is systematically excluded.

This type of conflict often needs reconciliation, because the game has a tendency to break away from the expected procedures. Winning tends to become addictive, and enterprise and competition regularly tend toward greed and vindictiveness and away from production and cooperation. The reconciliation that is needed here is a common commitment to continue to adjust procedures and forms of interaction in the direction of more cooperative relationships, after first recognizing that a separation has taken place and that it was not positive.

Reconciliation of group conflict of the second and third types seems almost impossible. With regard to the second type, there is no space where the Hatfields and the McCoys—or what is an equivalent situation, opponents in the abortion issue—can meet peacefully. Reconciliation is thought to mean compromise, and there can be no compromise of basic values. With the third type, where structural exclusion is the cause of division, the first challenge is to bring people to recognize the reality of the structure itself, which is often as far from conscious recognition as is the air we breathe. The surplus resources of the powerful are hidden from the eyes of the marginal. Not only is there no space where the groups might meet to be reconciled; the mist is so thick that often there is not even a recognition that reconciliation is needed.

One cannot simply select the time for reconciliation in such a context or project a schedule of its stages. Those who undertake a ministry of reconciliation have to stay alert for those special opportunities that must be seized as teaching moments or moments of consciousness-raising or recognition. After recognition is reached, the reconciliation process remains extremely difficult, because the distance between the parties is so great, because it is so hard to see such a distant "enemy" as a child of God, as someone worth dying for, and because the threat that reconciliation poses to the structure itself is disorienting. The challenge is to find or create some space where the antagonists might meet, some way to bring them together, perhaps for cooperative work on a project of mutual concern. Ask, for example, why the Christian Churches must continue to do separately all those things they can do together.

Absence of Guilt

One thing common to each of the three types is that the group and the group members do not feel guilty about the division between the groups. If they recognize the split at all, they may regret it and wish it were not so, but generally they experience a sense of their own innocence or rectitude in the situation. This absence of guilt not only diminishes the chances for reconciliation, but raises questions about the suitability of the sacrament of reconciliation for the purpose.

The third level is the farthest from any sense of guilt, because the groups typically cannot see anything that is wrong. For example many Christians approved the closing of many mental health institutions five to ten years ago. That policy was intended to save money, to reintegrate the marginally ill back into a more normal environment, and to direct resources to alternate forms of care for the mentally ill by means of halfway houses and outpatient services. In many cases, however, the alternate forms of health care did not develop, because they were seen to be in conflict with other values, such as the need to husband scarce resources and to protect some vaguely perceived quality of "neighborhood life." These decisions were largely responsible for the new army of the homeless that walks our city streets. They are a ghostlike metaphor for how well-intentioned public policy can drive large numbers of people to the margins of society.

In this case it is possible to point to the causes of the problem, something which is not always true of third type divisions. But it is not possible to find guilt; responsibility, perhaps, but not guilt. In other words certain policy decisions are seen in retrospect to have been responsible for the problem. Those who devised, sponsored, executed, supported, and approved those policies are also seen in retrospect to be responsible. But it is not as though there was an intention to banish a whole class of people, already on the fringe of society, to a twilight zone between life and death. The responsibility is the inadvertent responsibility of the sleepwalker.

In a type-two division there is typically less ignorance and more righteousness, but, again, no guilt. The parties are convinced of the correctness of their position and of the virtue of their group.

The problem with the first type of division is that it is difficult for Americans to see that accumulation and control are no more virtuous in public and business life than they are in interpersonal relationships. In fact competition is often thought of as the engine that produces those values that make life worth living. Insistence on cooperation and participation, it is feared, will work against the virtue of enterprise and inevitably lead to those scarcities that are the source of basic divisions. I must concur with Paul Roy's observation in the previous chapter that the culture in which we live is a large source of the problem. It requires us to stand apart from each other, to compete, and finally to win or lose. There is no sense of guilt connected with such a philosophy or with playing by the rules of the game that channel activity in the worlds of work, business, politics, and government.

A Sacramental Reconciliation

In each type of split it is common to find groups of people damaged, disoriented, marginated, losing hope. Not all lost sheep are sinners, we discover; they may be the losers in the normal game we are all in, whose rules and processes build up barriers between us while at the same time distracting the (relative) winners from the conditions in which the (relative) losers are left to spin out their lives.

While there is usually no sense of guilt when group opposes group, nevertheless reintegration of the mentally ill homeless into the larger society is desirable, even required, as is reconciliation of the abortion issue opponents and of two groups of parents that have come near to blows over the school budget.

An early step toward reconciliation in each case may be to have people recognize responsibility without at the same time feeling guilty. People would come to the point of saying: things I did, or did with my group, or approved of as my group did them, *caused* a damaging situation which I would not have wanted, had I known it would result; and the future depends on us all developing an attitude that says the present cannot be allowed to stand, that a new future is called for, and its reality depends on a continued effort to change the attitudes and procedures that caused the past damage.

Thus the traditional understanding of the sacrament of penance does apply to the reconciliation of groups in its central requirement of a firm purpose of amendment and in the need that each person repent of past responsibility for damage to other people's lives. Where the traditional understanding does not fit so well is in its requirement of an admission of guilt.

The present shape of the sacrament of reconciliation is not a good match to the reconciliation of groups for a second reason. It continues to emphasize the individual and the personal. When a group seeks reconciliation, each person in the group confesses the same thing: what *we* have done as much as what *I* have done, a common regret that the group's past actions have unwittingly added to the dimensions of social sin and personal hurt. It is a painful admission that is better when shared by all the members of the group present with each other, both for mutual support and to make repentance effective for the future. In fact it is not likely that a series of individual private confessions can really represent a turning of the *group* in a new direction.

Real effectiveness suggests the presence of the other group too, so that people can face their former adversaries and weep together, forgive, begin to trust each other, and swear cooperation for the future. Each group's witnessing of the other's purpose of amendment is itself a key link in the chain of reconciliation. The penitents will actually see and feel the distance between them being shortened.

Reconciliation does not happen automatically, any more than private confession guarantees the penitent for the future. The rite of reconciliation can only be a strong link in a chain of events that gradually bring the group members to recognize their social situation for what it is and their unwitting responsibility for it. Those events will have to continue after the rite itself, because compassion for the other group only slowly overcomes the distaste and fear.

Like the Eucharist a rite of reconciliation of groups could both express a degree of unity already achieved and mark a reaching for a unity not yet achieved. Total resolution of conflict need not be a prior requirement for the "sacrament" to take place. The rite itself could be a key moment in the process of restructuring the relationship, that is, a public visible swearing of each group to the other in the midst of the larger Church community, whose delegated representative assures both groups of the community's and God's pleasure with them, future support of them, and blessing and healing of them.

A Countercultural Experience

It is as difficult for a group as for an individual to see clearly that it has allowed the world to squeeze it into its mold without knowing it (Rom 12:2) and that the destructive nature of competition, control, and power has taken it over after all, with the inevitable and unanticipated result of divisions and broken lives. When the past has become as familiar as a comfortable pair of shoes, it is hard to see that past as evil, to break out of silence and ambiguity to name it as such, and to turn back toward a following of the Lord Jesus.

A reversal of what once seemed so right is disorienting, opening up a door into an unfamiliar and dark experience. The darkness may not be temporary either, like something that passes as one becomes accustomed to the world beyond the door. Often enough the passage is not through a door at all, but toward a thin band of light that shines only on the horizon, on the fringe of the familiar world that one must leave, a light that tries to rise against the dark ways of the present world but hardly can increase at all. You can imagine the Gerasene demoniac (Mark 5:15-20) shaking at the prospect of entry into the new world opened up for him by Jesus, knowing his lack of resources and support. You can also imagine the uncertainty of a bishop resolving to put away the vertical pattern of control and determining to walk into the world of collaboration, openness, and consultation, no matter where it leads.

You can also imagine the price to be paid by a group of Americans attempting to wrench themselves out of the familiar ways of thinking and acting, that is, from competition to cooperation, from power to service and empowerment of others, from exclusivity to inclusion, from upward mobility and position to downward mobility and a preferential option for the poor, from a sense of rectitude to a recognition of personal responsibility. Repentance is refusing to live within the old structures and accepting the unfamiliar and threatening new world. By many standards the option is simply crazy; by any standard the option is costly.

The cost is not just in the option for life on the fringe, but in the recognition that true reconciliation requires action. The reconciliation will be a sham if one of the groups must remain in a permanently inferior position relative to the other. That may require action to deal with the structures of the society and its ethos, just because those structures hurt people and are the source of injustice. It means first of all a resolve to stop complicity and move, perhaps gradually, to extricate oneself and enable others to do likewise. It means assistance to victims and, finally and most importantly, some activity oriented toward a reconstruction of the system in grace.

With this common sworn commitment to act, the reconciliation enters still more into the realm of the sacramental, because the purpose of amendment becomes firm. The swearing for the future makes God's presence still more visible, makes hope real and opens the way for the promised grace to become effective.

It should not be surprising that the complete reconciliation of groups is hard to achieve, and therefore rare and always fragile. It is for that reason that a rite of reconciliation of groups may be valuable: to lift people up together, to enable them to see a new future that might indeed be achieved and is certainly worth reaching for, and to enable them to see that they are not alone. It may be more memorable and effective once it is linked with some expression of the dream, an exchange of the greeting of peace, the common saying of the Our Father, and a sharing of the bread and wine.

Conclusion

There is no reason to be optimistic about the chances for reconciliation of groups, especially if the division between them derives from ideological commitments or social structures. Nor is there reason to believe that the sacrament of reconciliation is especially useful for the reconciliation of groups, given its traditional private and individual structure and its emphasis on the confession of personal guilt.

Nevertheless, the difficulty of reconciliation is no reason to put reconciliation aside. It is, one might reasonably assert, the very center and purpose of Christian life. And the sacrament both instructs us about what the process of reconciliation has to be and offers a model that can be adjusted to make the reconciliation a present reality. It points to the need for group members to recognize that they are in a sinful situation, even though they are innocent of blame, and that the future is in their hands.

These steps do not happen in quick succession; they are pieces of a fragile process. When the groups are ready, at the right moment when trust begins to master fear, a public ceremonial disowning of the past and swearing for the future promises to make God's grace present and effective. This is especially so if the support of a wider community is there to share the cost and the burden of making an alternative future actual.

3. RECONCILIATION AND FORGIVENESS:
A THEOLOGICAL REFLECTION

Peter E. Fink, S.J.

If there is a single proclamation about the identity and mission of Jesus of Nazareth that shocked and scandalized the religious leaders of his day, it is the one embedded in several of the recorded healing stories, namely, that Jesus had the power to forgive sin. "Who can forgive sins but God only?" was the astonished cry in Luke 5:21[1] to which Jesus offered the physical healing he accomplished as proof that he did indeed have the power to forgive sin. If there is a single proclamation about the identity and mission of the community of believers that formed the Church of Jesus Christ which would continue to be a shock and a scandal, yet at the same time be an enduring challenge and Word of good news, it is that the mission and power of Christ was passed on to his followers. "If you forgive the sins of any, they are forgiven," the risen Christ announces to the disciples in John 20:23, echoing the promise of the discourse at the Last Supper: "He who believes in me will also do the works that I do, and greater works than these" (John 14:12), and the words of Paul in 2 Cor 5:18: "All this is from God, who through Christ reconciled us to himself and gave us the ministry of reconciliation."

Reconciliation and forgiveness stand at the heart of the Church as the enduring gift of God to believers and the enduring mission of the Church to the world. These are not merely words to be spoken, but realities that are to be brought about in the lives of people. Reconciliation speaks of a healing of division and the reestablishing of communion and harmony among people and within them. Forgiveness names the conditions for such reconciliation: allowing God to be God, allowing others to be free, and allowing oneself to be humbly and honestly human before both God and others. In whatever ways the Church acts to bring about reconciliation and forgiveness, it enacts its deepest truth as the *sacrament* of Jesus Christ and fulfills its Christ-given mission to all people, believers and unbelievers alike.

Within the Catholic community we speak not only of the mission and ministry of reconciliation and forgiveness, but of a distinct *sacrament* that brings this mission and ministry to public, liturgical expression. As is true of all such liturgical action, the sacrament of reconciliation and forgiveness "is thus the outstanding means by which the faithful can express in their lives, and manifest to others, the mystery of Christ and the real nature of the true church" (CSL 2).[2] It is, in whatever liturgical form it might take, a living embodiment of the reconciling and forgiving Christ. Christ is present in this liturgical action; in the Word that is proclaimed; in the minister or ministers who serve to embody his forgiveness; in the assembly gathered for worship, prayer, and reconciliation; and in whatever concrete gestures of forgiveness and reconciliation the assembly may enact among themselves (see CSL 7).

These two dimensions of reconciliation and forgiveness, as mission and ministry of the entire Church and as the liturgical ritual which embodies and accomplishes that mission and ministry, form the focus of these theological reflections. Of concern, therefore, is both process and sacrament. The context in which these reflections occur further determines the shape they will take. Paul Roy and Denis Woods have both expressed challenges from the arena of the human sciences which theology and liturgical *praxis* cannot ignore. While it is true that a theological reflection on the sacrament of reconciliation and forgiveness has its own agenda to fulfill, these challenges and the four ritual alternatives which dialogue with the human sciences has generated add a further dimension to that agenda and reflection.

This chapter will unfold in four parts cast as reflections. A first reflection will examine the human dilemma of division both within and among people that yearns for the forgiveness and reconciliation of Christ. A second will explore the Gospel Word which speaks to this human condition as good news and the sacramental action which effectively proclaims this Gospel Word. A third will examine the general process of conversion and forgiveness, and a fourth will identify four specific factors that present themselves to the contemporary Church in the wake of the Second Vatican Council.

Reflection I: The Need for Reconciliation and Forgiveness

The terms "reconciliation" and "forgiveness" address both a personal and a communal need for healing. When they are used for an individual, they hold out the promise of inner peace, harmony, and wholeness in the face of one's inner disruptions and divisions. When used among people, whether for two or for many, they speak of a coming together, a unity, a community. In either case they point to division and the path to overcoming division. Each of these will be considered in turn.

DIVISION WITHIN

Paul Roy has spoken of the process of growing up and has given some of the psychological factors involved in the process. Let me take a complementary tack here and begin by naming from the arena of pastoral experience some of the things within each of us as individuals that need to be reconciled. These divisions, which require some kind of healing and reconciliation if we are to be whole human persons, can exist on at least three different levels, and it is important to name them and understand them so that we can pursue the right path for their undoing.

The first level is more properly psychological than religious, though it is not without its religious dimension. Some examples can serve to identify this level of division within. Imagine someone who is so controlled by a deep insecurity that he or she is forced to latch onto others in fierce dependence, perhaps to use and exploit them for personal ends, perhaps even to destroy others to keep from being destroyed. Imagine someone who needs to gain power over others in order to assert self-worth, or to keep others enslaved to one's own expectations of them. Consider someone whose inner self-hatred forces him or her to drink too much, argue with loved ones, or destroy relationships that are truly important. Most, if not all of these, do have a destructive interpersonal result, but they are rooted in a division that is intensely intrapersonal.

This kind of inner division is simply unhealthy, and the first task of reconciliation must be towards inner health. Religious motive may well serve to help the person towards a more healthy style of life, but the primary path to reconciliation must be medical and not religious. The behavior involved in each case is destructive, and that alone cries out for some kind of healing. But the root of the behavior is an unhealthy self-possession, and that is what needs to be addressed.

I would not want to speak too quickly of sin on this level of division. This is not because there is no sin, but rather because an unsophisticated sense of sin could prevent the proper path to wholeness from being pursued. To address the behavior and never get at the source, for example, might leave the person controlled and better behaved, but not truly forgiven or reconciled. Roy is correct in asserting that the psychological processes need to be taken on their own terms and not too quickly transferred over into the moral religious arena.

On the other hand, I would not want to dismiss the reality of sin altogether. Simply to excuse all on the basis of psychological illness could rob the person of a prime motive to seek a psychological cure, and would in fact go contrary to the cure that is desired. The point is that there is destruction here, and it is always sin to choose destruction or passively to acquiesce in it. The moral demand on all of us is to help each other seek and to seek for ourselves healthy and constructive patterns of living. If, as in these instances, the path to wholeness demands medical treatment, such treatment must be included in the process as an integral part of the Church's mission and ministry and recognized to be an integral part of the sacrament which embodies that mission and ministry.

A second level of division might be called "institutional-religious." This particular level of division belongs to the arena of structural problematic which Denis Woods named as one of the categories of group alienation, but what I have in mind is an effect on individuals rather than groups. The issue here is to belong to the community of the Church, which has its own discipline, rules, and regulations, and yet not always to live up to that discipline and those rules and regulations, as one happens to understand them. This phenomenon, which is probably the most common experience of "sin" among Catholics, is complex and calls for more than simple admonition to proper behavior.

At times it is a case of misinformation that needs to be cleared up. How often does someone confess "missing Mass on Sunday because I was sick!" I was once asked to give absolution "for the next three weeks" because someone was going on vacation and would not be near a Catholic church. This is clearly not a question of sin at all. Sometimes it is rather a case of not really understanding the rule or regulation or not really being convinced of it. It is on the books, and should claim some kind of allegiance, but deep down the person does not see the point of it all. Hence arises a division between what "the Church teaches," and what the individual believes and does. Finally it may at times be a case of simply not being able to do what the Church asks of an individual. This could be the classic "habitual sin" of the older textbooks, which would more properly belong to level one above. It could be a confrontation with one's fragile humanity in the face of a proposed ideal, or more complex conscience decisions such as to practice artificial birth control or partake of the sacraments while living in an "irregular" marriage.

The process of forgiveness and reconciliation will on this level call for many things. It could, as in the first instance, require education to the fact that the Church does not and cannot bind one to the impossible, and that there are many occasions when people can simply excuse themselves from the demands of the Church's discipline. Or perhaps as in the second case, it could call for the delicate task of conscience formation, where the discipline of the Church is explored for its power to claim allegiance, if and to the extent that it can indeed claim such allegiance. Or in the final instance it might require on the part of the penitent recognition both of the Church's humanity and the penitent's own and call for the ability to forgive humanity on the part of each. Whatever it does require, however, must be likewise required of the mission and ministry of a reconciling Church and of the sacrament which expresses and manifests that mission and ministry. No simple and certainly no facile response will do justice to the healing that is called for.

There is a third level of division, which I will call the moral-religious. It is here that sin is most deeply experienced and that the need for God's gracious forgiveness and reconciliation is most deeply required. This is different from the situation where I do what I want, though it may clash with the tenets of the Church's discipline. It is also different from the situation where, in Paul's words, I do what I do not want to do and do not do the things I really want, or where I experience my own fragile humanness. Here I do exactly what I want to do, but the doing goes against something deep within me. It may show itself in a variety of choices and actions that are called sins, but it is in fact something deeper than these. It is choosing against one's own conscience, not simply violating an external law. Here the "wrongness" is known, not because someone else tells us, but because something nags at us and something is violated from within. The experience of sin on this level is a profound religious experience, and the reconciliation it calls for is likewise a profound religious experience. Unlike the first level, which I have said is more psychological than religious in nature, and which is best served if the psychological paradigm is given its proper primacy, this level is just the opposite. It is more religious than psychological, and it is the religious paradigm, rather than the psychological, which will prove to be the more accurate guide.[3] What is called for is nothing less than conversion, repentance, and a transformation to new choices that are more in tune with the law which God has written on the human heart.

These are some of the inner divisions that need healing and reconciliation if we are to know the inner peace and wholeness that is the forgiveness of Christ and the reconciliation of God. Readers may well be able to identify themselves somewhere on one or several of the levels named. The purpose of naming them, however, is to illustrate from within the pastoral experience of the sacrament of reconciliation the range of inner division that is exhibited, its complexity and variation. It is also to remind ourselves what experienced confessors quite quickly discover, that no simple or single solution to these divisions is adequate, nor indeed is any simple or single ritual enactment of the liturgical sacrament.

DIVISION AMONG PEOPLE

The need for reconciliation and forgiveness also arises in the arena of interpersonal relationships. This includes certainly the harmful effects that redound toward others from the personal divisions mentioned above. Psychological pressure, ignorance, and personal malice do most often bring injury upon others, and this injury ought not be minimized or swept away. In a world where personal wholeness is at the same time interpersonal wholeness, the personal and the interpersonal are necessarily and deeply implicated in each other. In a very real sense all personal sinfulness is destructive interpersonally as well, and reconciliation *within* must somehow include reconciliation *among*.

The concept of restitution, classically applied as a point of justice in instances of theft (restoration of material goods taken) or slander (restoration of one's good name defamed), captures this relationship between personal sin and its interpersonal effects. The alcoholic, for example, who not only damages himself or herself by unhealthy behavior but also brings injury to others, needs both medical treatment to restore healthy patterns of living and intervention to heal the damage done to relationships. Only then can full reconciliation and forgiveness be realized. Conversely, this same person will need the healing support of others in forgiveness and reconciliation. One cannot be reconciled alone. This is but one example. The levels of personal division can yield many more in the realm of the interpersonal.

There is another kind of interpersonal division which is not in itself the product of evil, yet which can quickly become evil if one acquiesces in it, acts from it, and refuses to move beyond it. It is a negative that necessarily shows up in all interpersonal relationships as persons and groups are discriminated from each other. Here is a factor that both Paul Roy and Denis Woods identify, each in his own way. My own preference is to employ the language and thought of philosopher John Macmurray,[4] who explores this factor as a negative which is essential to all interpersonal relationships and yet potentially destructive of those same relationships if it is not overcome. He calls it the process of "withdrawal and return." It might well be called "alienation and reconciliation."

Macmurray uses the paradigm of the mother and child to illustrate this phenomenon of alienation-withdrawal. He describes the necessary resistance to its own desires which the child must experience from the mother in the process of becoming an individual. Refusal on the part of the mother to yield to the child's every demand results in negative feelings of rejection and alienation. Growth demands that the child move beyond them to see that, in spite of this resistance, the mother does indeed love and is indeed still good. In other words the negative, while necessary, is not final. It must be overcome and moved beyond by the power of a positive.

As a paradigm this mother-child relationship and the process of withdrawal and return contribute some understanding of the reality of social sin and help to illuminate the path to its undoing. Whether among persons or among groups, the negative is necessary for discrimination of one from the other. This in itself is good and vital for human growth. Yet if one chooses to remain in the negative alone and act as though the negative alone contained the total truth, destruction is all that can result. The choice to remain in the negative reinforces social sin and makes it personal sin as well.

The experience of resistance and opposition forces the person (or group or nation) to withdraw from the other into the realm of the negative. This is the realm of isolation, of the rhetoric of exclusion (we-they), of alienation. The challenge for growth, both for the person and the relationship, involves a return to the positive from the negative. Here is the key:

> If the return from the negative phase is to be completely successful, it is necessary that the dominance of the negative motive be completely overcome, and that the positive relation . . . be fully reestablished.[5]

This is the challenge of reconciliation, both for individuals and especially for groups.

John Macmurray insists that the return cannot be made from egocentric motives, that is, motives that are essentially grounded in self-interest. It can only be made from motives that originate *in the other*, that allow one to see the resistance as not alienating after all, but rooted in a deeper relationship which remains true in spite of the resistance. A return from the negative based on motives rooted in the negative cannot succeed in reconciliation. Only the lure of the positive can succeed.

In all kinds of interpersonal division, the image of the other is the key. Negative images breed alienation; positive images invite reconciliation. Negative images must be overcome if reconciliation is to take place. Reconciliation cannot be imposed by force, nor can it be achieved through motives that are exclusively self-serving. It can only be arrived at through a positive appeal from the other, which overcomes the negative and brings about reconciliation. It is true that self-interest may well require other forms of pragmatic cooperation, and, for a time that may be all that can be achieved. But such pragmatic cooperation is not yet the full ideal proposed in reconciliation, and eventually it may run aground.

The same may be said of personal divisions. Whether one is confronted with psychological pressure, ignorance, or choices of willful malice, it is the appeal of a positive image, now of oneself, that guides the path to wholeness. Other dynamics will often be necessary along the way to make reconciliation possible, such as medical treatment, education, and conscience formation. But these will not be finally sufficient unless some positive appeal can be supplied to overthrow the dominant grip of the negative.

A positive image of God, of others, and of oneself is the path to reconciliation and forgiveness. It is also the core of the Gospel

Word which is addressed to us in Christ and the deepest truth that is enacted in the sacrament of reconciliation. To this Gospel Word and sacramental act we now turn.

Reflection II: Word of God and Sacrament of Christ

The good news revealed by Christ and carried on by the Church is that in Christ all divisions, both personal and interpersonal, are overcome, and all evil—social, structural, and institutional—is rendered finally without power. "For our sake he (God) made him (Christ) to be sin who knew no sin so that in him we might become the righteousness of God" (2 Cor 5:21). It is not enough that this Gospel Word be spoken; its truth must enter the fabric of human life and reap the effect it so boldly proclaims.

Division *within* and division *among* cry out for an undoing, and it is central to the mission and ministry of the Church to serve this undoing of sin. The ritual of reconciliation and forgiveness manifests and accomplishes this mission and ministry, for within the ritual the Word is proclaimed and the truth of that Word is acted out. The aim of this second reflection is to examine the Word that is proclaimed in Jesus Christ and how that Word is enacted in the sacrament which is his anamnesis. This will be done in light of the range of divisions that inflict themselves on human life, and will be at the same time an exploration of the path to forgiveness and reconciliation.

As a first step we will look at the life of Jesus of Nazareth and the choices he made to shape that life, one which is said to be "without sin." Jesus is the Word we proclaim and God's revelation of the path to human wholeness. In fact the very reason that we look at Jesus and try to understand the choices he made is that his choices are the choices we must make if we would find wholeness and peace. In the choices Jesus made toward his own life and the choices he made toward the lives of others, the secret of true reconciliation is to be found. As a second step we will then examine the claim this life of Jesus makes on anyone who would be his disciple and explore how the sacrament of reconciliation expresses and leads us into the power of that claim. Since both the life of Jesus and the sacrament of reconciliation respond directly to our deepest need for forgiveness and reconciliation, both will be explored as yielding the positive that is needed to overthrow all divisive negatives.

Along the way the term conscience will be used and that reality identified and named. It may be spoken of as "the God within," or "one's true self," or "one's own integrity." However it is named, the attempt is to focus on the reality which the Second Vatican Council named as the very dignity of the human person and the norm according to which all will be judged:

> In the depth of human conscience we detect a law which we do not impose on ourself, but which holds us to obedience. Always summoning us to love good and avoid evil, the voice of conscience can when necessary speak to our heart more specifically: do this, shun that. For we have in our heart a law written by God. To obey it is the very dignity of men and women; according to it we will be judged.[6]

In dealing with the reality of sin and reconciliation, this voice of conscience within and the freedom to hear and act according to it are central.

Jesus, the Word of God

The life of Jesus, as it is recorded in Scripture and understood in the light of faith, is a life at once thoroughly human and yet singularly immune to the power of evil, which distorts and destroys humanity in the rest of us. Because his life is a true human life, Jesus can speak to us. And because it is free of all the distortion that evil can bring, his life can reveal to us what true human life can be. Because his life is a true human life he can proclaim that true human life is not beyond the reach of men and women, but is within their grasp. And because it is free of all the distortion that evil can bring, he can reveal the secret of that grasp.

If we are truly to listen to the life of Jesus, we have to abandon any notion that his life was radically different from our own. Such exclusion of Jesus from the human race would simply silence anything he has to reveal to us. It is a well-known danger of the proclamation of Jesus' divinity that it can falsely lead us into a crypto- or not so crypto-docetic denial of his true humanness. Jesus was no stranger to the divisions that beset us. If he were, he could not be our savior. As Gregory of Nazianzus proclaimed long ago in speaking of the human condition, if it was not assumed, it was not redeemed. It is a truth that was set forth even earlier in the Letter to the Hebrews: "He can deal gently with the ignorant and wayward, since he himself is beset with weakness" (5:2).

Jesus' life was a true human life. Like ours it had to be shaped and chosen. Like ours it was beset by the force of evil which tried in vain to conquer him. In this alone he is unique among all men and women upon the earth: he succeeded where by ourselves all the rest of us must fail. He is called the sinless one, not because he had a power that made him superhuman, but rather because he possessed and was possessed by the secret of true human life. This secret is the Word he speaks to us. And its name is *Abba*. The life of Jesus was guided by and obedient to One he named *Abba*, and this *Abba* was found within him. This *Abba* guided and shaped his life. This *Abba* spoke the Word he listened to in the choices he made for his life. This *Abba* is the secret of true human life, and the revelation of Jesus to us all is that this *Abba* dwells within us too.

In his book entitled *Poverty of Spirit*,[7] Johannes Metz gives some hints into the reality of *Abba* and the relationship that existed between *Abba* and Jesus. He explores the story of the temptation in the desert as holding the secret to the choices which shaped Jesus' whole life. The story itself unfolds immediately after the account of Jesus' baptism, and the revelation of Jesus' own identity before God. "Thou art my beloved Son; with thee I am well pleased" (Mark 1:11). In the desert temptations the terms of that relationship and of the life that will be shaped by it are set forth. The tryptic, "If you are the Son of God . . . ," seeks to dictate from without what shape the life of Jesus would take. The triple response on Jesus' own part negates that path in favor of one more true to himself. In effect Jesus says, "I am the Son of God, but God alone will tell me and I alone will choose what that will mean."

If read against the description of conscience given above, the terms of the temptation are clear. On the one hand, there are the many voices outside himself, even perhaps the voice of his own dreams, wishes, and expectations; on the other, the voice deep within, where his integrity and his deepest identity are to be found. To listen to the voices outside himself is to say "no" to that deepest identity and truth. To listen to the voice inside is to be faithful, to say "yes."

When we say that Jesus was "obedient unto death," we are naming the claim that this inner voice—conscience, *Abba*— had upon him. It is that voice to which he was obedient. Likewise when we say Jesus was without sin, it is this faithfulness to his own human life that is meant. If Jesus holds up a pattern for us, a path to wholeness and inner peace, it is this pattern of obedient surrender to his own deepest truth, that inner core of his own life where he met and named the God he came to reveal. It is a pattern for us, because his deepest truth is ours also.

Because his path of obedient surrender is the way to wholeness and peace, we must ask what it was that allowed Jesus not only to hear but faithfully to follow this voice of *Abba*. We could say, as so often is said, that "he was God," and by that remove him from our own human arena once again. It is tempting, because since we are not God, that bold proclamation would nicely get us off the hook. But such is true neither to the revelation of Jesus Christ nor to our own human life. The more honest answer is that Jesus listened to this inner voice because he trusted that it was from God, and he trusted that the God within could indeed be trusted. Trust: it is this trust that is pressed out in his life and especially in his death, and it is the condition for obedience to be possible.

For the Jewish Jesus the God who made covenant with Israel is the source of that trust. God's promise to be faithful provides for Jesus the hope that his own obedience will be vindicated. Trust in the faithfulness of the Lord is the dominant theme of the Hallel psalms sung during the Passover meal. It is a dominant theme in the Jewish faith which claimed and shaped Jesus' life. But whatever the resources Jesus himself had that enabled him to trust this voice of *Abba* within him, he has become for us in the resurrection our primary path to the same trust. He has become a new sign of the covenant of God, the sign that with him we too may now trust this voice. His trust has been vindicated and God's covenant confirmed. As the sign of the new covenant, Jesus himself in his life and death reveals to us the profound power of this trust, its possibility, and its necessity along the path of human wholeness which is redemption.

Trust is what Jesus reveals to us about God. His life, death, and resurrection tell us that this kind of trust not only can be made but needs to be made if sin is to be overcome. Sin is at its deepest surrender to all the other voices that would seek to shape our lives, and is thereby a profound violation of the integrity and truth of each human person. It could be what others want us to be; it could likewise be the voice of our own demands and expectations. Whatever, it is not the voice of *Abba* which is placed upon our heart. It is not the one voice which alone brings wholeness and peace.

The path along which Jesus wishes to lead and guide those to whom he says, "Follow me," is the path of trust and faithfulness to the God within. We cannot imitate him in externals, which must be so different for us in our time and place. We are not asked to imitate him in externals. True discipleship demands that we imitate him much more deeply, in his listening, his trusting, and his following what he has heard. He does this by being for us the sign of the covenant. He does this by holding up before us the God whom he trusted as a God we too can trust. He does this by asking us to heed the voice within, just as he did, and to be faithful to our own human life even as he was faithful to his. As sign of the covenant, Jesus presents the positive that can overcome all negatives.

The three levels of division noted above are all about this voice of conscience, this voice of *Abba* within us. The division itself is rooted in an inability to trust and follow and a need rather to follow other voices and seek one's security there. Each level of division presents its own unique challenge. The first asks us to make sure that the inner voice we hear and heed is indeed a healthy voice, and not one imposed by psychological pressures and distortions. If it is not healthy, it cannot be the true voice of conscience which is heard. The second challenges us to make sure that the inner voice is informed by truth and value and honesty. If it is misinformed, shallow, or based on a denial of one's own humanity, it is not the voice of God within. Finally the third challenges us to make sure that the inner voice of *Abba*, once it is tuned in and attended to, is indeed listened to. This demands generosity, trust, and a deep inner freedom. Through it all we need to remember that when Christ calls us to wholeness he calls us to health, to adult faith and commitment, and to freedom.

The appeal which Jesus makes to us to say "yes" to our own human life is not only a personal appeal; it has implications on the interpersonal level as well. The relational patterns established by Jesus and recorded for our own instruction reveal the same profound respect for the integrity of each human life that he had for his own. Nowhere is Jesus presented as seeking to dominate or control others and shape them according to his own will and desire. He took friends and enemies alike and gazed on them with profound respect for who they were, invited them to wholeness, wept over their resistance, yet resisted only those who themselves resisted their own deepest truth.

In saying "yes" to his own human life, Jesus likewise said "yes" to the human life of each person. He looked beyond the surface, where the negative would emerge, to a profound depth of each person, which was the positive that overwhelmed the negative. His command to love as he loved is a command to look beyond the surface. His many parables that spoke of and illustrated the worth of each person called notice to the positive beyond the surface. His loving surrender to the structures and institutional forces that made his rejection and death inevitable proclaimed that beyond all negatives there was a positive that could conquer them all. "Father, into thy hands I commit my spirit" (Luke 23:46). *Abba* is the positive that is beyond and within all negatives.

The Word which Jesus reveals and proclaims to us as the victory over sin and death is deeper than all negatives and is the positive which brings reconciliation both within and among all people. In Macmurray's words withdrawal and alienation, however inevitable and necessary they be, are not the last word. It is the return of reconciliation that is the true nature of things. "God was in Christ reconciling the world to himself" (2 Cor 5:19). "If anyone is in Christ, he is a new creation; the old has passed away, behold the new has come" (2 Cor 5:17).

This new order of things is the truth and the hope in which and because of which we Christians continue to make the anamnesis of Jesus Christ. Remembrance holds before us the positive of God, the positive of each human life, the positive of our own human life. Remembrance proclaims the deepest truth of all human life, which is Jesus Christ and which in turn can set right all the distortions of sin and lure us to have the same mind in us that was in Christ Jesus (see Phil 2:5), to shape our lives as he shaped his.

Anamnesis of Jesus: the Sacrament of Reconciliation

The sacraments of the Church are enacted in anamnesis— remembrance—of Jesus Christ. This is especially true of the Eucharist, which is not only the primary sacramental act of the Church but the prime sacrament of reconciliation as well. The Eucharist is the *anamnesis* of his sacrificial life and death, and it continues to make present his sacrifice and its victory over sin. It is likewise true, however, of the special sacrament of reconciliation which proclaims and effects deeper union with Christ in his sacrifice and with the community of people formed at the Eucharistic table. "The liturgy is thus the outstanding means by which the faithful can express in their lives, and manifest to others, the mystery of Christ and the real nature of the true Church" (CSL, 2).

The sacrament of reconciliation proclaims the positive in the face of the negative. Citing the command in Acts 2:38 to preach forgiveness to all people, the instruction accompanying the new *Rite of Penance* clearly sets forth the positive nature of this liturgical act: "Since then the church has never failed to call men from sin to conversion and by the celebration of penance to show the victory of Christ over sin."[8] The sacrament of reconciliation is not enacted in order that God *will* forgive sin, but rather because in Christ God *has already* forgiven sin. It is a celebration of the positive not the negative. Everything which Jesus reveals about God and the possibility of trust, and about human life in which God sees the positive not the negative, is acted out in sacrament by the assembly gathered, and thus it is "expressed" in their lives. The hope is not that God will forgive, but that we will know forgiveness. The hope is not that God will reconcile, but that we will forgive others as we are forgiven, and thus be reconciled both with God and each other. We act out the positive revealed by Christ in hope and expectation that this positive will overcome the negatives within us and among us and thus conquer all that is sin in our midst. This kind of faith and hope is the stuff of true anamnesis.

The task here is to see how the Word spoken and revealed by Christ is effectively enacted in the sacrament of reconciliation. Since the primary sacrament of reconciliation is the Eucharist, this should be examined first. This is so in order that the special sacrament that brings the mystery of Christ to bear consciously and deliberately on the negatives of sin may be seen as related to and enlightened by the Eucharist.

Structurally the Eucharistic act is made up of four parts: Word, offertory, consecration, and communion. Each of the parts has a goal and a purpose, and together they draw those who enact them toward the relationship which the Eucharist itself proclaims, namely, relationship in the Body of Christ. The goal is towards *koinonia*, communion, which is itself the achievement of reconciliation.

In the Eucharistic action the Word presents the assembly with the story of God's presence and activity in the life of Jesus Christ, a story which the assembly itself is called to be part of. The goal of the liturgy of the Word is to invite generous offering and trust. The offertory is the assembly's first response to the Word, a giving over of the members' whole lives to the God revealed in Christ. In the consecration God takes what is given over and speaks to all the words once spoken upon Jesus himself: "You are my beloved." It is a word of election and of transformation. Food is indeed transformed by this word, but for the purpose of transforming a people. Food becomes the Body and Blood of Christ, that in St. Augustine's words we might become what we eat. Finally the communion reveals the fruit of God's consecration: we turn to each other in peace as sisters and brothers in Christ.

In the Eucharist the covenant of God is boldly set before the assembly, as is the obedience of Christ to *Abba* that is his sacrifice. In the Eucharist the God of Jesus is made present as one who has been trusted and as one who can be trusted. In the Eucharist God says "yes" to Jesus Christ and with him to all whom he gathers to himself. God says "yes" to each of us, and that is forgiveness. God says "yes" to those who are around us, and this is the positive that invites and makes possible reconciliation and communion.

The special enactment of reconciliation and forgiveness is not independent of these dynamics of the Eucharist. It is in fact bringing them forward in the face of evil and sin. Remember that the proclamation of the Word is integral to the sacrament of penance even as it is to the Eucharist. With perhaps a focus more finely tuned to the reality of sin and division, the Word nonetheless presents us with the story of God's action in Christ, a story which we are called to be part of. Still it invites generous offering and trust, but in this case, most specifically, the offering of our evil, our division, and our sin. The act of confession, whether it be done individually or in common, by word or by gesture, is a response to the Word proclaimed, an "offering," a giving over to a God who can be trusted. The prayer and proclamation of absolution, again in whatever form—be it declarative, "I absolve you," or imprecatory, "May God forgive you," or some combination of both as in the current *Rite of Penance*—is in fact a consecration which changes sin into non-sin and renders all forces of evil to be without final power. God says "yes" to Jesus Christ and to all who are gathered with him. God says "yes" to each of us in the very acknowledgement of our sin and in the boldness of offering even sin in worship and in praise. God says "yes" to those around us, and in that "yes" gives us the motive and power to say "yes" to each other. The "yes" of God to each of us is forgiveness. The "yes" it empowers us to give to each other is reconciliation.

In both the Eucharist and its specific articulation toward sin which is the sacrament of reconciliation, what is expressed by the whole gathered assembly is the affections of Christ. What is expressed is the reality and truth of *Abba* within each of us. What is expressed by us gathered and acting is the fundamental choice of Christ toward his own life, which in turn becomes our choice for our lives as well. What is expressed finally is the stance of Christ toward all people, a stance born of a power to see the positive within them that overcomes all negatives that divide.

The sacraments, of course, do not offer instant cures and should not be expected to do so. They are actions that work in a gentle way to bring about the realities they proclaim. They take time and frequent doing, for all they can do is appeal to us in our freedom and invite us to yield to the working of God within us. It is conversion and the transformation of heart that the sacrament seeks to serve, and this conversion follows its own dynamic which needs carefully to be understood. The Word proclaims the truth about God, each other, and ourselves which is the positive that can overthrow the negative. The sacrament enacts the truth of that Word and, for a moment at least, allows us to taste the victory of the positive over the negative. Neither, however, can violate the freedom of the human heart. They can only serve the path of conversion and transformation. They cannot force or impose it.

This awareness takes us to a third reflection to understand the process of conversion and transformation which Word and sacrament seek to bring about.

Reflection III: The Process of Conversion and Transformation of Heart

The process of conversion is the victory of the positive over the negative and the return which is both forgiveness and reconciliation. The transformation of heart proclaimed in Word and enacted in sacrament is likewise the victory of the positive over the negative and the return of forgiveness and reconciliation. In this third reflection conversion and transformation seek to be illuminated and understood as a human process in itself and as one which is served by sacramental ritual. Rather than attempt an analytic presentation of the process, I will offer instead a collage of pieces, each of which will contribute some insight into the conversion and transformation process.

A first piece of the collage is the penetrating study of the role of the imagination in the process of healing the mentally ill offered by William Lynch in his *Images of Hope*.[9] Lynch contrasts the phenomenon of hope with that of hopelessness. He contends that a major dilemma that binds the mentally ill is a feeling of entrapment, which is in turn an inability to imagine a way out. If entrapment is the path of the hopeless, the hope that heals can offer release from entrapment.

Lynch's description of hope, especially in contrast to the pit-falls of hopelessness, is instructive as we try to imagine the process of conversion and the role of liturgical ritual in that process. True hope, first of all, is the imagination of the real. It is not "wishful thinking" or the idle "hope against hope" of popular usage. True hope presents a real alternative to one's situation and presents it in such a way that the path forward is indeed possible. To present the impossible is to feed rather than release from entrapment.

A second characteristic of hope, according to Lynch, is that it is a collaborative effort. Hope seeks help; it *imagines with*; it is not, as is commonly supposed, a purely interior device.

> What happens in despair is that the private imagination, of which we are so enamored, reaches the point of the end of inward resource and must put on the imagination of another if it is to find a way out.[10]

The path of healing for the hopeless requires the aid of another's way of imagining in order to stretch one's resources beyond one's own private limits.

A third characteristic of hope is that it is not unlimited or absolute in its range. Lynch forestalls this illusion with stark insistence:

> Not everything can be hoped for. Nothing leads to more hopeless-ness than the naive theory that everything can indeed be hoped for.[11]

This is consistent with what was mentioned above, namely, that the path forward must be possible. One does not offer help to the hopeless if the alternative set before them in fact cannot be hoped for. It is precisely the mistaken supposition that all things can be hoped for that reduces true hope to the polite and useless level of wishful thinking.

A final characteristic of hope suggested by Lynch is its intimate relationship to wishing or desire. If one is apathetic or simply una-ware of the entrapment one is caught in, hope is not possible. If a person does not wish for anything, nothing that is offered will capture the imagination as a desired and indeed needed alternative. Integral, then, to the path of healing is the ability to touch the level of desire with the appeal of what is offered, so that the person will not only be vulnerable to its power but will actually pursue it.

These four characteristics of the hope that heals, namely, a real option offered by others that is both possible and desirable, can serve as a first insight into the process of conversion and transfor-mation where true hope is essential to the task. It can also be taken to name the task of liturgical ritual in the process of conversion, forgiveness, and reconciliation. Ritual activity inserts people in an imaginative framework, and the sacrament proposes to the imagination the way for human life and relationship that is revealed by Christ as alternative to the way of sin. It is not a pious wish that leads people to the sacrament or that urges the assembled Church to enact it. It is and can only be the deep conviction that faith in Jesus Christ does in fact undo the reality of sin. Without the conviction that sin is indeed transformed by surrendering it to Jesus Christ, ritual enactment of that transformation will be a hopeless as well as a useless act.

Beyond that, moreover, Lynch cautions the liturgist against so arranging the ritual that it minimizes the force of the alternative imagination by almost reducing it to a private, internal resource. A case can be made against the exclusive enactment of private confession in this regard, especially where the ministerial assistance of the confessor is restricted to a few words of advice and the formula of absolution. On the contrary, Lynch's advice would urge as normative the full, communal enactment of the sacrament, where the faith of others visibly and tangibly gives strength to the truth which the ritual displays and invites people into. Indeed it further urges ongoing realities within the community's life structures which will continue to reinforce the imaginative power of Christ's healing alternative.

Finally Lynch's reminder that what is truly hoped for must be both possible and desirable names two further dimensions of the task involved in giving sacramental shape to conversion, forgiveness, and reconciliation. For the first, neither in catechetical instruction nor in the ritual itself, ought we lead people to expect "instant disappearance" of that which they name as their sin. Such would certainly be to feed a hopeless project. On the theological plane, to be sure, sin presented to God in Christ is by that very act transformed into non-sin, as the word and prayer of absolution ritually articulate and accomplish. Such is not the case, however, on the experiential level, where the effects of sin and the tendencies toward sin follow a different time line towards their undoing. The sacrament is not magic, nor a washing machine, nor a feat of alchemy. Time is always a factor in the healing it proclaims. For the second the ritual must appeal to the apathetic and the unaware, not by hurling merciless guilt trips upon them in the hope of awakening "true repentance," but by setting out in attractive and appealing imagery the conviction that Christ's way proclaimed in Word and enacted in sacrament is in fact more interesting and more humanly true than the way of evil and sin.

Appeal to the positive, show that it is possible as well as preferable, draw on the strongest statement of the Church's imagination and not the most restrictive, and indicate that the way of Christ is real and not some pious wish. This is the contribution William Lynch brings to an understanding of the process of conversion and transformation, and of the sacramental ritual which serves that process.

A second piece of the collage is supplied by Paul Ricoeur, who instructs us on the passage from what imagination sets before one as an appeal coming from *without* to an internalization and affirmation of what is imagined. In theological terms this passage is the goal of the conversion process and the transformation it effects.

In his investigation of the human will, *Freedom and Nature,*[12] Ricoeur seeks to understand freedom's response to the assault of human limitation. It is the instinct of freedom, as he has analyzed it in the tension between the voluntary and the involuntary, to say *no* to all forms of limitation. Freedom seeks to be absolute, freed from the constrictions of its incarnation in human beings. Faced, however, as it inevitably must be with the reality of human limitation, freedom responds with the "no" of refusal, a refusal which is itself freedom's destruction.

Ricoeur seeks to move beyond the destruction of freedom to its liberation from its own illusions. He urges freedom to realize itself as "an only human freedom."[13] The path he traces out is that from refusal to consent, a consent which cannot be forced but which must be "wrested from" refusal. Consent, as he puts it, "does not refute it, but transcends it."[14]

The path from refusal to consent is by way of transcendence. For Ricoeur this means that freedom must come to terms with its true relationship both with facticity, which obstructs and limits it, and with transcendence, from which freedom derives its own illusions of absoluteness. Along the way there are two traps that can thwart freedom's true liberation: a stoic resignation to one's limitation, and an euphoric absorption in the wonders of transcendence such that one's facticity is blithely forgotten or ignored. The first is the inevitable result of a starting point that looks squarely at facticity, yet with no resources to reach beyond its limitations. Resignation is all that can be wrested from refusal. The second is the temptation when one looks to transcendence without giving serious thought for the human encasement which transcendence wears. One is tempted to leave behind what is embarrassing. True consent, of which the liturgical equivalent is *Amen*, is only wrested from refusal when in the face of transcendence and drawn by its wonder and its power, freedom can claim its facticity as its own. Transcendence, as the positive, lures beyond the negative of facticity, but only after facticity has been thoroughly owned. This is what Ricoeur calls "an only human freedom."

It is the appeal of poetry or poetics, to use Ricoeur's term, which invites and brings forth consent.[15] The ways of poetics must be observed. Poetry and the poetic imagination do not coerce their outcome in the way, for example, that logical argument or declarative prose might do. Poetry can only make an appeal and await a decision, a choice, a surrender of the one to whom the appeal is made. Its first contribution is to *humble*. It does this by inserting the person into a world of imagining that is large enough to relativize one's immediate perceptions and so render those perceptions vulnerable to alteration. One's own concerns, however they may seem urgent and all-important in themselves, need to be seen as finally not all that important. Or perhaps another way of putting it, one's interpretation of things, which may be limited and restricted, needs to be opened up to other possible interpretations which are more freeing and rich with greater possibility. At the same time poetry humbles in order to *heal*.[16] It invites one to enter its truth and be drawn to interiorize that truth. This truth is impressed upon the person *as that person is*, and the yes given to it—consent, Amen—brings it within and thus accomplishes the transformation that was hoped for.

In complement to what was learned from William Lynch, Ricoeur urges upon our attempt to understand conversion and its transformation that the forgiveness offered by Christ in the Church is an only human forgiveness. The reconciliation which may be brought about by the Church's mission and ministry, and indeed its sacrament, is an only human reconciliation. The healing of sin which Christ works through the Church's action and prayer is an only human healing. The passage to that forgiveness, reconciliation, and healing is akin to the passage from refusal to consent.

The two traps which Ricoeur names along this passage, which ultimately may thwart its successful completion, have their counterpart in the passage to reconciliation. The first is a resignation to one's sinfulness which, in Lynch's terms, is finally hopeless. "God loves me in spite of my sins," expresses this sullen resignation. The second is a resplendent rehearsal of the mercies of God that plays down, distorts, and finally effectively denies, the hard reality of one's sins. "What matter my sins in the face of so generous a love!" Neither touches sin as it is, and neither accomplishes the yearned for transformation.

On the path to the Amen of consent, one must indeed be humbled, both by the evil of one's sins and by the magnificence of God's love. But our sins seek to be healed and not simply diminished in importance. For true forgiveness and reconciliation it is necessary that our sins be claimed in all their horror and presented in trust to God's merciful love. Only if God's love can be consented to by one who can claim his or her sins in surrender, can the sin itself be transformed into non-sin and the process of healing advanced.

Sacramentally this means two things. First of all the ritual must both present the mercy of God in its fullness and give ample attention to the claiming of one's sins in all their negativity. God's love remains the primary horizon against which all else takes place. Yet the claiming of one's sins in honesty and integrity is necessary to draw one into that horizon of God's love. It does not serve the healing mercy of God to play down out of some false sense of compassion and/or embarrassment the ugly reality that sin really is and the harsh reality that these are indeed *my* sins. Honesty with the truth of one's sin is needed if we will take the greater truth of God's love seriously. The second implication for sacramental reflection and practice is that the laws of poetics must govern the ritual enactment. Time must be given to the appeal of God's mercy in whatever imaginative forms that mercy is presented. The healing of poetics is a contemplative act, which appeals, invites, and gently awaits the freedom of consent. It is here that not only the text of the ritual, but even more the style and manner of the presider and other ministers, as well as the entire liturgical environment and tempo and rhythm, must be seen as integral to the accomplishment of sacramental healing.

A third contribution to the task of understanding conversion and its transformation can be gleaned from those who, in a variety of ways, have examined and named the process as it unfolds in other human arenas. Two will be looked at here: one drawn from the experience of the Spiritual Exercises of St. Ignatius Loyola and the other from the experience of death and dying.

The Spiritual Exercises of St. Ignatius are divided into four sections or "weeks" of prayer, each bringing the retreatant into contact with a specific dimension of the mystery of Christ. The first week is of primary concern here, because its main focus is on the passage from sin to forgiveness. William Barry has given a detailed description of this process drawn from his own experience as a retreat director, and it is this description which can further illuminate the sacramental task.[17] In this passage the sinner is placed imaginatively before the intense love of God made manifest in the crucified Christ and is drawn by the constant vision of that love through three interior movements. The first is a desire to be rid of one's sins and indeed to be without sin at all. The second, representing the intrusion of reality on that otherwise noble desire, faces one with the realization that such is not possible, at least not in any immediate or obvious way. The third movement brings the liberating awareness that one need not be without sin to gain this freely given and all-embracing love of God. It is the grace of the first week to be drawn to a point of living freely and in peace with the knowledge that one is a loved sinner.

Elisabeth Kübler-Ross gives a parallel view in her study *On Death and Dying.*[18] Her now familiar stages are not without their similarity to the experience of one before one's own sinfulness. Death and sin alike meet first with denial and a dynamic that isolates and closes in on oneself. In time this may lead to anger, intense bargaining, and a resignation that breeds depression and sadness. William Lynch would call this last "hopeless"; Paul Ricoeur would see it as a "stoic resignation" that forestalls consent. If such were the final stage of the process, the outcome would be dismal indeed. Kübler-Ross, however, names one final stage, which her own hope guides people into. The movement in this final stage is from resignation to acceptance and peace.

The echoes of both Lynch and Ricoeur are clear in these two brief descriptions of the passage of conversion and transformation. Yet they do not simply repeat but rather advance our understanding of the conversion process in one important respect. In William Barry's three inner movements there is a kind of logical inevitability that leads from the first to the second. Given enough time the second will simply break through. Likewise in the stages of death and dying there is a logical inevitability that denial will lead to anger, anger to bargaining, and all—out of exhaustion if nothing else—to sad resignation. In both cases, however, this is not true of the final stage, which in each is the transformation and healing. There is something gracious about this final stage, something of *grace*. Acceptance comes as *gift* in the face of resignation. Release from the

frustration of helplessness before one's own sinful condition comes as *gift* from the God who embraces and loves without limit. The dynamic shifts, and one must simply await from another that over which one has no control.

There is a point in all Christian ritual when one must stand helpless before the freedom of God. We act with the confidence of faith but never with the smugness of control. The ritual can itself guide people through steps that follow upon each other with some kind of logic. At some point, however, the dynamic must shift to something like awe, expectancy, or humble submission. Ritual, like poetry, must humble in order to heal. In the Eucharist consecration is such a moment, as is the anointing and confirming attached to baptism and Christian initiation. Within the sacramental enactment of reconciliation and forgiveness, this moment of humble submission is the prayer of absolution, though one may well question how successfully our rituals have served this necessary affection. The genius of the Western Church in its employment of a declarative form of absolution, has been to serve the embodiment of God's forgiveness and its ongoing incarnation in the living Church. Its weakness has been to obscure or omit altogether the sense of humble expectancy which the Eastern form of imprecation more successfully expresses. Both are of course needed. The first emphasizes our service; the second, God's free gift.

One final piece of the collage remains. The presentation of sin to God for its transformation can be read as a rite of passage, and studies of such rites can help us understand, respect, and indeed serve this time of humble waiting.[19] The specific dynamic that is useful is that which is embraced by the three stages of separation, liminality, and reaggregation. The first, separation, is easy enough to understand. The child is given up by the mother and entrusted to the place of the "mysteries." There is a sense of loss in that the child is no more. The third stage, reaggregation, names the return of the child, now an adult, to the home, the village, and the tribe. In an act that certainly goes beyond the literal evidence, the "child-who-is-no-more" is treated as an adult. Each of these stages exhibits its own proper behavior. If in the first stage the task is to let go and in the third stage, to relate in a new way, in the second stage of liminality there is needed yet a third style of behavior. There one does *nothing*; one simply *entrusts*.

The application of these three stages of "passage" to the process of conversion and transformation is quite fitting, for in the assembly sinners to be reconciled go through a form of passage. On the part of the sinner, sin itself must be "let go," a phrase which far better describes the act of worship which the sacrament is, than "acknowledgement," or even "confession." Sin is placed with Christ before the Father for its transformation into non-sin, a transformation which only the Father through the Spirit can bring about. It is a move to liminality. One does nothing; one simply entrusts. On the part of the assembly, there is also a "letting go," a giving over of the sinners in faith, in hope, and in worship to God. They too finally do nothing but simply entrust. The vindication of that trust comes in the third stage where sinner receives his or her life back and where the assembly receives the sinner back, now to act in a radically new way: sin forgiven and sinner reconciled. Reality entrusted to the mystery can never be the same, even though it may appear to be so when it returns. The new behavior that follows, that in fact authenticates what faith and hope proclaim, must simply take for granted that the transformation has occurred. Forgiveness and reconciliation belong to the stage of liminality but are only known in reaggregation.

This final voice adds two things to our understanding of the process of conversion and transformation proper to the sacrament of reconciliation. First of all, it gives yet another way of seeing the process itself, one which the Church must serve, both in its mission and its sacramental act. One does nothing; one simply entrusts and then proceeds in the conviction that God has indeed acted. This profound act of entrustment must be called forth and served. In the second place, it draws attention to the importance of the new behavior which must follow such entrustment. If people act as if nothing has happened, can we really say anything has? To paraphrase the Apostle Paul, how will anyone believe if no one acts as if they believe?

This third reflection on the process of conversion and transformation has proceeded by way of a collage. Several voices have been called upon to illuminate a process which does not proceed by logic alone. It is a poetic process, an imaginative process, one which preserves and respects human and divine freedom and one which is itself a form of passage. It involves our images of ourselves, of others, and of God and the transformation of those images from all that is alien to Christ's revelation to all that he himself has revealed. Such a transformation is the work of conversion; it is the work of the sacrament of reconciliation as well.

A final reflection returns us to the sacrament and in particular to four factors which significantly influence both the understanding and the practice of reconciliation in the postconciliar Church.

Reflection IV: Four Factors That Affect the Sacrament of Reconciliation in the Postconciliar Church

A first factor which must be taken into account in any present and future enactment of reconciliation is, of course, the understanding of sin, which is deeper and more fundamental than individual actions which may manifest it. Charles Curran made this point quite clear some years ago:

> Mortal sin can never be just one isolated action. Since mortal sin involves the total orientation of the person, the laws of human psychology remind us that man does not ordinarily make such a drastic change by just one isolated action. Rather the change begins to occur gradually in the person through a number of smaller and less important actions.[20]

This now commonplace observation must be taken seriously in designing and reflecting upon the sacrament of reconciliation. Sin is not something instantaneously incurred, nor is it instantaneously healed. Sin is rooted in the choices which people make, and it shows itself in a variety of behavior manifestations. The simple naming of such actions, in whatever detail as to "number and species" accompanied by some word of absolution, cannot get at the reality of sin nor produce in any effective way the healing sin calls for.

In the waning years of preconciliar private confession, many questioned its effectiveness on the basis that they would only do again the deeds they mentioned so frequently. Ironically this complaint is not an argument against the sacramental act but rather a testimony to the need of its regular enactment. What needs to be remembered is that sacramental healing is a slow process of conversion and not an isolated act of forgiveness, and the proper view of the sacrament must be within that process of conversion. Just as sin grips the human heart slowly, so its undoing in the grace of Christ must be a slow process. The liturgical action cannot replace or absorb the full conversion process, nor can it replace either the wisdom or the strategy that the reconciliation of both persons and groups might require. Yet it is essential to the process. It will be necessary in the future to abandon the sense of one enactment of the sacrament "doing it all" and begin to see many sacramental enactments in relation to each other and to the full human process of reconciliation they serve and guide.

A second factor that must affect the future of this and other sacraments is a renewed understanding since the Second Vatican Council of the mode of sacramental effectiveness. While it was recognized and affirmed by St. Thomas Aquinas that sacraments achieve their effects by signifying (*sacramenta significando efficiunt*),[21] it nonetheless remained in the background of Scholastic theology. This forgotten principle of sacramental causality has been set in bold relief in the Constitution on the Sacred Liturgy:

> In the liturgy the sanctification of man is manifested by signs perceptible to the senses, and is effected in a way which is proper to each of the signs (CSL, 7).

The mode and method of the act of signifying must be taken into account in any discussion of sacramental causality and a fortiori in any evolution of sacramental ritual form.

To bring about sacramental healing and forgiveness "by signifying" is a specific way of making something happen. An image is set in human consciousness which begins to alter that consciousness. Rarely is the image so overpowering that it immediately stamps out all other counter images and achieves instant transformation. Of course such sudden and radical conversions are possible. They are not, however, the norm. The process of conversion and the process of signifying are of a piece. The sacramental act is an act of signifying, and it is *as such* that it helps to bring about its intended healing and forgiveness.

A third factor that will guide the Church into its new phase of sacramental activity is the renewed attention the Second Vatican Council gave to the inner dynamic of ritual activity and the importance of the full and active participation of all the people in it. This is a further acknowledgement of the role of ritual in the process of conversion and transformation. Ritual does not simply signify in the purely cognitive sense of posing to human consciousness an alternate way of understanding. Ritual engages people in a network of signifying activity, the very doing of which involves them in a new way of feeling and acting as well as understanding. What is signified in the sacramental act is not simply a forgiveness, a healing, or a reconciliation that may happen somewhere along the journey of conversion and transformation. What is signified is the very results of that conversion, tried on, tasted, and perhaps even enjoyed for a bit. The doing of the sacrament allows its promise and its outcome to be realized and experienced (*ex opere operato*), provided, of course, one is open to the dynamic of what one does and puts no obstacle in the way (*ex opere operantis*).

The Constitution on the Sacred Liturgy employs an intriguing metaphor for performing sacramental action. Through the liturgy "the work of our redemption is exercised" (CSL, 2). It is a metaphor that allows and urges us to view sacramental acts in relation to each other in the way one might view physical exercises. Not much weight is put (or lost) on any one exercise. It is precisely the regular and oft repeated pattern that accomplishes the hoped for effect—slowly, steadily, but quite definitely. So it must be with sacramental "exercise."

A final factor that must be taken into account in the shaping of this reconciling ministry of the Church is the recognition that all sacraments are liturgical activities, that is, activities of the whole Church hierarchically gathered. For the sacrament of reconciliation, this reminder draws attention to an odd conflict within the official instructions that accompany the current ritual forms. Liturgical activity, according to the Council, is always communal action, so much so that:

> Whenever rites, according to their specific nature, make provision for communal celebration involving the presence and active participation of the faithful, this way of celebrating them is to be preferred, as far as possible, to a celebration that is individual and quasiprivate (CSL, 27).

In spite of this, however, the current ritual preserves the priority of individual confession and absolution.[22] It would seem—at least from one voice present in the current ritual—that the sacrament remains envisioned as an act between penitent and confessor alone. From all that has been said, however, it should be clear how detrimental it would be to the sacrament and to the process of reconciliation if this private view of the sacrament is not radically enlarged upon.

If the liturgical nature of this sacrament is given its proper stress, however, the ministry of reconciliation, both in fact and in sacramental enactment, is regained as belonging to the whole community and certainly to more than the ordained priest alone. The priest remains presider over the assembly's prayer and action, but he never absorbs its totality into himself. Others in the assembly have an important role to play in the reconciliation of penitents, and that role needs actively to be pursued and liturgically expressed.

Concluding Remarks

Thus we come to the end of these reflections. In addition to the challenges posed to liturgical *praxis* by Paul Roy and Denis Woods from the human sciences, theology too has some challenges to pose. Chief among them is the challenge to extend the healing power of Christ—that is, part of the ministry and mission to reconcile which has been entrusted to the Church—to the whole range of sin and division that inflicts itself upon the human race. Christ is neither narrow nor stingy in his power to forgive and reconcile. Neither should the Church be narrow or stingy. A second challenge lies embedded in the recognition of reconciliation as a liturgical act, that it requires and should have many ministers for its many ministries. These should not be relegated to the arena of "preparation" for the sacrament; they should be recognized as integral to the sacrament itself. A final challenge lies in the human process that is conversion and transformation of heart. Any liturgical form that might be employed to enact Christ's reconciliation and forgiveness is and must be in service to that profoundly human process. Liturgical ritual does not present a process of its own independent of the ways of an incarnate Christ in the flesh and blood lives of people. It remains wedded to the proclamation of the Word. It remains an unfolding in sign, symbol, and human interaction of that Word. And the Word proclaimed and enacted in liturgical ritual is, and always must remain, the Word-made-flesh.

Footnotes

1. See also, Luke 7:36-50; Matt 9:1-8; Mark 2:1-12.
2. *The Constitution on the Sacred Liturgy*, 2. All quotations from Vatican II documents are from *The Documents of Vatican II*, ed. W. Abbott (New York: America Press, 1966). The Liturgy Constitution henceforth cited in the text as CSL.
3. An excellent discussion of the difference between the psychological and religious paradigm in counselling and spiritual direction is presented by Dr. John Allen Loftus, S.J., in the *Bulletin of the Guild of National Catholic Psychiatrists*, 1982.
4. See John Macmurray, *Persons in Relation* (Atlantic Highlands: Humanities Press, 1979 [orig. 1961]) chapter entitled, "The Process of Withdrawal and Return."
5. *Ibid.* 99.
6. *The Pastoral Constitution on the Church in the Modern World (Gaudium et spes)* 16.
7. Johannes Metz, *Poverty of Spirit* trans. J. Drury (New York: Paulist, 1968).
8. In the Introduction to the *Rite of Penance*, no. 1.

9. William Lynch, *Images of Hope* (Notre Dame: University of Notre Dame Press, 1974).

10. *Ibid.* 23.

11. *Ibid.* 47–48.

12. Paul Ricoeur, *Freedom and Nature: The Voluntary and the Involuntary*, trans. E. Kohak (Evanston: Northwestern University Press, 1966).

13. *Ibid.* 482.

14. *Ibid.* 466.

15. *Ibid.* 468.

16. *Ibid.* 478.

17. William A. Barry, "The Experience of the First and Second Weeks of the *Spiritual Exercises,*" *Review for Religious,* 32, 1973, 102–109.

18. E. Kübler-Ross, *On Death and Dying* (New York: Macmillan, 1969).

19. For a liturgical application of this "rite of passage" approach, as well as additional bibliographical references, see Robert Hoeffner, "A Pastoral Evaluation of the Rite of Funerals," *Worship,* 55 (November 1981) 482–499.

20. Charles E. Curran, *Christian Morality Today: The Renewal of Moral Theology* (Notre Dame: Fides, 1966) xvi–xvii.

21. For an excellent study of this neglected dimension of scholastic theology, see J. F. Gallagher, *Significando Causant: A Study of Sacramental Efficiency* (Fribourg: The University Press, 1965).

22. "Individual, integral confession and absolution remain the only ordinary way for the faithful to reconcile themselves with God and the church, unless physical or moral impossibility excuses from this kind of confession." From the *Introduction* to the *Rite of Penance,* no. 31.

4. HISTORY OF THE SACRAMENT OF RECONCILIATION

Peter E. Fink, S.J.

The term "sacrament of reconciliation" in its narrowest and most familiar sense refers to the liturgical ritual of the Church by which a penitent, through the mediation and ministry of a priest-confessor, is granted absolution and forgiveness in the name of Jesus Christ and thereby restored to union with God and the Church. In a broader sense, however, it refers to the Church itself and to all the activities of the Church, liturgical and otherwise, which aim at the undoing of sin and division and seek both human wholeness for individuals and true communion among peoples. As already noted in the theological chapter in this volume, the Church as sacrament of Christ is missioned to continue Christ's own reconciling work until it is brought to completion in the Kingdom of God. This is the sacrament of reconciliation writ large.

The history of the sacrament in the narrow sense has been fairly well researched and is readily available in both popular and scholarly works. A brief bibliography is appended to this chapter. The history that encompasses the larger sense of the sacrament, namely, of the Church in all its actions that promote healing and reconciliation within and among peoples, is in fact the history of the Church itself, at least in its brighter moments when it has displayed in countless people and accomplished in countless ways the reconciling mission of Jesus Christ.

The history presented in this chapter is not simply a summary presentation of materials available elsewhere, and it certainly does not pretend to be a summary of the history of the Church. Two particular points of focus guide this presentation: the challenges presented by the human sciences in the chapters by Paul Roy and Denis Woods and my own theological reflections; and the project of alternative futures which the rituals that follow hope to advance. It is as much a reflection on the history of reconciliation as it is a presentation of the history itself.

Woods is correct to point out the intensely individual nature of the liturgical forms of the sacrament as they are and have been in use in the Church. The sacrament has been enacted primarily— one might even say exclusively—toward the forgiveness and reconciliation of individual penitents. It has included the individual in relation to and in solitude before God, the individual in relation to other individuals, and the individual in relation to groups. It has not addressed the situation of alienation among groups nor that of a group towards an individual. Thus a sketch of the history of the sacrament narrowly understood can only honestly stand in dialogue with the challenges which Roy and I have presented. We will have to look at some broader than liturgical activities of the Church in its larger history if the challenges which Woods presents are to be located and engaged.

The Origins of the Sacrament of Reconciliation

It has been customary within Latin theology, at least since the thirteenth century when the various sacraments were named and analyzed with systematic precision, to look to the New Testament and if possible to events in Jesus' own life for clues to the origin of the sacraments. The point of departure for the sacrament of reconciliation was twofold: Jesus' own claim to forgive sins (as in Luke 5:18-24) and his post-resurrection commission to Peter and the others to bind and to loose, what is called "the power of the keys" (see Matt 16:15-19 and 18:18). This, of course, locates the ministry of reconciliation within the restricted arena of the apostles' successors, namely bishops and priests. A complementary text, which has not received its just due in terms of the origin of the sacrament, is found in 2 Cor 5, where the whole Church community is named as that which is entrusted with the mission and the ministry of reconciliation.

At any rate this Latin conception of the origin of sacraments, namely, as located specifically or at least generally in the life of Jesus, is itself currently under examination and critique. It tends to sug-

gest, if not demand, something radically new, originating in its totality with Jesus of Nazareth and not rooted firmly in familiar Jewish
faith and practice of Jesus' day. This view of things does not stand
up well to either biblical or liturgical scholarship, both of which
have been able to trace for all the sacraments, albeit in many cases
sketchily, a gradual evolution in both form and meaning from the
faith and the *praxis* of Jesus' own Judaism. This recovery of continuity rather than radical discontinuity, or rather discontinuity
within the context of a more fundamental continuity, has opened
up a deeper understanding, not only of the "how" question—how
sacraments began—but more importantly of the "why" question—
why they continued in ever new and more deeply understood ways.

A more promising place to begin to understand the "coming to
be" of the sacrament of reconciliation is the promise given in both
Jeremiah (31:31-34) and Ezekiel (36:26-28) of a new age to come
when God will not only establish a new covenant with Israel but
will make it possible for Israel to keep it. The context of the prophets'
announcement is hardness of heart, because of which Israel could
not be faithful. But God would alter that by placing God's own
heart, God's own spirit of faithfulness, within the people.

It was this promise and this new age that the Jewish disciples
of Jesus latched onto to understand both the resurrection of Jesus
Christ and the sense of newness they themselves experienced in its
wake. The new age had dawned. The new covenant had been forged,
with Christ himself its sign and pledge. The spirit of God was named
as God's own gift to those who believed. God's spirit was indeed
placed in the human heart.

It was a spirit of inner transformation, the softening of hard
hearts, and a new possibility for people to be faithful to the covenant God made with them. Since God's law was written on their
hearts, fidelity to God was at the same time fidelity to their own
deepest truth. Hardness of heart, the inability to be faithful to God's
truth and to their own, named for the Israelites the reality of sin.
This new spirit, this new power to be faithful, ushered in the conquest of sin. Sin undone, sin vanquished, sin forgiven—these all
spoke the same reality. In Jesus Christ the new age has dawned,
sin is forgiven, and the spirit of God is placed in human hearts.

Paul Roy has spoken of the psychological process of growing
up, of coming to adult wholeness, of latching onto one's deepest
truth and embracing it as one's own. Seen through the lens of the
psychological paradigm, it is a psychological process. This same

process, however, if seen through another lens becomes the theological process of redemption. It is the work of God's own Spirit leading men and women to their own deepest integrity and truth. Roy suggests that the psychological process must be taken into account in any theological reflection on reconciliation. And he is correct. Theology does not address a different process; it names the deepest reality that hinders it, namely sin, and the deepest resource for the process to succeed, namely, the action of God through faith in Jesus Christ.

The Christian imagination was captured by the truth of this new age and associated the forgiveness of sin first with that ritual act which expressed and sealed one's faith in Christ and occasioned God's gift of Spirit. "What shall we do?" the crowd replied to Peter's proclamation of God's new deed. "Repent and be baptized each one of you in the name of Jesus *for the forgiveness of sin*, and you shall receive the Holy Spirit" (Acts 2:37-38). The death and resurrection of Christ ushers in the new age whereby sin is forgiven. For the post-resurrection Church baptism, which incorporates men and women into that death and resurrection, remains the initial (initiatory) act for the forgiveness of sin.

In time, as they continued "in the breaking of the bread" (Acts 2:42), as they proclaimed God's deeds in Christ in the meal *berakah*, and as they drew the connections between God's presence to them in meal, Christ's fellowship with them in meal, and the Spirit enlivened in them through the breaking of the bread, this act too was named *"for the forgiveness of sin"* (Matt 26:28). God's Spirit given in baptism was continually invoked and celebrated in the remembrance act which would become the Eucharist. If baptism was the initial act for forgiveness of sin, Eucharist would be the ongoing act where the truth of that forgiveness was received and deepened.

Why then the need for yet another act "for the forgiveness of sins?" That is the question which Latin theology seemed never to ask. And it could not as it is being asked here, because it began with the sacraments *as given*. If we start, however, not with the sacraments as given but with a human need that cries out for a Gospel response, then the answer can only be that baptism and Eucharist did not suffice to deal with the realities with which the Church was presented. It seems that the early Church had to discover what Paul Roy names as psychologically obvious and what I pointed out as theologically obvious in my treatment of conversion, that the process of transformation is a human process that takes time. It takes time and a continual entrance into the truth of God's action in Christ for that transformation to succeed.

Yet here is a dilemma and the reason why yet another act "for the forgiveness of sins" had to occur. The truth of baptism, perceived from the beginning, though only gradually accepted universally, is that it cannot be repeated. If sin never showed itself among the baptized, then this single act would have been enough. Yet in the humanness of it all, sin did in fact manifest itself. The truth of the Eucharist is that it is for the forgiveness of sins provided one can partake of it. In fact in the early Church, Eucharist was seen to be the sacrament of reconciliation where sin did not violate Eucharistic communion and require excommunication. If such damage to the Eucharistic communion had never arisen, the Eucharist would have remained the sacrament of reconciliation for all. Yet such damage did occur. What then?

What was to be done for those whose very actions separated them from the place of true forgiveness except to lead them back to that place of forgiveness? In its origins the act of reconciliation was a restoration to Eucharistic communion. However it spelled itself out—and the very nature of the damage required several steps toward its undoing—the completion of the process was restoration to Eucharistic communion, and in that restoration the sinner found once again God's forgiveness in Christ. Reconciliation with the Church was reconciliation with God. And this was true both for those few who needed to be restored to communion and for those many who remained in communion. The Eucharist itself was the place of reconciliation with the Church and with God.

The History of the Sacrament of Reconciliation

In the evolution of it all, the Eucharist was the primary sacrament of reconciliation, with the act of restoration—or second baptism as it was sometimes called—serving to lead one back to that Eucharistic communion in the same way that baptism initiated one into it. As long as the unity of those actions was preserved, the truth of the Eucharist as completion of reconciliation and forgiveness could be maintained. History reveals, however, that this unity was not preserved.

The first thing that affected the history of the sacrament of reconciliation was an evolution in Eucharistic understanding. While the accent on unity of the Eucharistic assembly is strong in the second-century Didache prayers and somewhat strong in the third-century Anaphora of Hippolytus, by the fourth century it is almost entirely replaced by concern for personal growth and holiness and even more forcefully by the focus on transformation of Eucharistic food. With the loss of unity as the prime reality of the Eucharist, the Eucharist could no longer be seen as the primary sacrament of reconciliation. The focus of reconciliation shifted to the act of restoration, which had to be completed before the Eucharist could be participated in. Whereas originally Eucharist completed the restoration and was the reconciliation, the intrinsic link between the restoration and the Eucharist was broken. The sinner was restored to the *possibility* of the Eucharist not to the Eucharistic reality itself. It is a subtle distinction, perhaps, in its initial phase but one which had serious consequences for the history to follow.

A second thing to affect the evolution of the sacrament of reconciliation was a shift in focus from sin as hardness of heart in *all its manifestations* to those *specific sins* which required this act of restoration by the Church. These were the "serious sins," the ones that called for special notice. Inevitably they would become in the popular mind the only sins that really mattered.

This shift is not unrelated to the shift in Eucharistic understanding just mentioned. Once again, as long as unity was held as primary for Eucharist, this third act "for the forgiveness of sins" was only required of those whose sinful acts violated that unity. All other sins were touched by God's forgiveness within the Eucharistic action itself, where unity and reconciliation were God's primary gifts to all. As unity disappeared as the primary truth of the Eucharist, it could no longer serve either to identify what sins in fact excluded one from it or to accomplish the reconciliation they required. As a result other sins, which might be judged to be serious by some other standard, were gradually added to the list of those which required reconciliation, and this BEFORE one could partake of the Eucharist. It mattered little that these sins might be more personal in nature than interpersonal.

Inevitably the reality of reconciliation shifted from the Eucharist to this auxiliary act, so that it would become the sacrament of reconciliation *in itself.* Lesser sins to be sure still found forgiveness through the Eucharist, but even here the accent became different. Forgiveness was less and less imaged as inner transformation through God's indwelling Spirit and more and more as a relational act between God and the sinner. The sense was that God would see Christ and therefore embrace the sinner. Forgiveness became an extrinsic act rather than an interior experience.

A full picture of this evolution would require far more space than this chapter allows. Development, particularly in the Latin West, of extrinsic theories of redemption rather than those which stress inner transformation would have to be explored as well as the significant loss, again in the Latin West, of the Holy Spirit as God's indwelling and transforming power. Even though this cannot be done here, it is important to name, however impressionistically, this major shift in the understanding of sin and its implications for understanding the act of forgiveness. As more and more sins become the material for this act of reconciliation, the scope of human sinfulness as it might be touched by the forgiveness of God ironically narrows. From the hardness of heart which prevents human beings from realizing their deepest truth with and before God, sin becomes sins, those first which by their very nature excluded one from the Eucharist and increasingly those which were taken to be "serious" disruptions of one's relationship with God judged by another standard altogether.

Against this backdrop the earliest form of the sacrament of reconciliation, commonly known as "canonical penance," gradually took shape. It evolved, as one would expect in liturgical matters, from the informal to the formal, from the simple to the complex. The Didache speaks of confession of sins in the context of the Eucharist "so that your sacrifice may be pure." Hermas speaks of "doing penance" on the way to reconciliation. Various documents of the second century know of public proclamations of excommunication with corresponding public proclamations of reconciliation, and at least in the case of Marcion, of public refusal to reconcile.

In the course of the first six centuries of the Church, and especially through the fourth to the sixth, the act of restoration to the Eucharist evolved into a full-blown discipline known as "canonical penance." It evolved with many variations to be sure, but in broad outline it followed the shape and patterns of Christian initiation. The accent was on penance, severe assignments of prayer and fasting designed to help the penitent reform his or her life. There was confession, sometimes to a presbyter, sometimes to the bishop directly, and the point of that meeting was to outline the path to restoration—the penance—that would ensue. When the penance was completed, the penitent would be publicly reconciled with a laying on of hands by the bishop, on Holy Thursday in the West and on

Good Friday in the East. Grades of penitents developed, so that one would return to the Eucharist in stages, even as the catechumens advanced to the Eucharist in stages. And prayers of intercession on the part of the whole assembly were included in the Eucharistic action to involve all in the community in this restoration of penitents.

Because canonical penance was directed at "serious" sinners, it would be difficult to link this piece of history directly with Paul Roy's process of "growing up." It is true that psychology knows of serious flaws in the human personality that inhibit such growth and employs intensive therapy in such cases. But Roy is talking about a process for the healthy as well as for those who are mentally ill, and intensive therapy is but a small if sometimes essential part of the process. Canonical penance is analogous to intensive therapy. It addresses the serious sinner, but leaves unaddressed the plight of the not so serious sinner. As I said above, that was the task of the Eucharist, but it was a task which increasingly the Eucharist was not able to address.

This inability to address the ordinary sinner with God's healing forgiveness is one of the limitations of canonical penance and no doubt one of the reasons for its eventual replacement by a form of the sacrament more tailored to individual growth and need. The major reason for its demise, however, seems to be a restriction which attended it. For reasons that some call rigoristic and others see as simply human, the "7 times 70 and more" of the Gospel became in fact a once only proposition. Canonical penance could be experienced but once. After that the sinner was left to the mercy of God, and the hands of the Church washed themselves clean. Because of this once only restriction and the severity of the penances that were assigned, people waited until the end of life, if at all, to begin the process.

From the point of view of human growth, either psychologically or theologically, it is as useless to restrict the healing process of reconciliation to the end of one's life as it was in an earlier phase to exclude people from the Eucharistic action. Yet there is a difference. In the case of the Eucharist, there was at least the possibility of a restoration. In this situation, however, the restoration became an entity in itself, now as inaccessible for human life as the sacrament to which it was supposed to restore one. How do you restore the process to the heart of human life where it may do some ongoing good? Obviously by removing the once only qualification.

The second major form of the sacrament evolved in a world which did just that. Born in the monasteries of the Celtic Church, private penance filled the huge gap which the regulations surrounding canonical penance opened up. The sacrament became again for the living and not simply for the dying. But as one might expect, this happened with some good news and some bad news.

The good news is that it was capable of responding not only to the growth process of each penitent, which must always be intensely personal, but to the dynamic of the process itself, which takes time and a constant placing of oneself within the truth which the sacrament proclaims and enacts. In addition, because the context of this new form of penance was that of spiritual direction, some attention could be focused on the differences between men and women, as Paul Roy suggested needs to be done. This latter, however, was very much a function of the quality of the confessor. Nothing in the ritual itself urged or fostered this.

The bad news is that it further separated the act of reconciliation from the Eucharistic assembly and hence fostered even more strongly the sense that penance restores one to the possibility of Eucharist and not to the Eucharist itself. A second bit of bad news is that the sacrament of penance was able to absorb into its own process not only serious sins but the whole range of human fault and flaw. It was, after all, about spiritual growth. While there is certainly a healthy side to this, it had the unfortunate effect of diminishing if not obliterating entirely the role of the Eucharist in spiritual growth. The Eucharist became more and more about the consecration of food, and the prayer for growth and faithfulness became quite secondary indeed. A final bit of bad news, perhaps the most serious of all, is the understanding of sin and forgiveness that was embraced. The Irish penitentials are notorious for assigning specific penances for an unimaginable range of human flaws, with the only distinguishing note among them being the duration or extent of the penance itself. Sin is accounted in varying degrees of seriousness, not by the specifics of the act nor even by the specifics of the effect but by the amount of penance that is assigned to it. A debt is incurred, and a debt must be paid for forgiveness to ensue. The only variable is the amount to be paid.

The development of this "economic," "quid pro quo" relationship between sin and forgiveness was indeed most unfortunate, for it separated totally both sin and its undoing from their own proper human processes. The payment of debt was the thing, and that was regulated by the code which prescribed it. Certainly this is farthest from either the psychological or the theological task of growth and conversion.

At first the pattern followed that of canonical penance in that confession led to penance and this when completed to a declaration of absolution. With multiple repetitions of the sacrament allowed, however, it became possible for the absolution to be delayed indefinitely as the amount of debt mounted. Should that occur, the sacrament would willy-nilly become yet again an end of life affair, a hopeless project, to recall William Lynch's phrase from my theological chapter. It would lead to despair rather than forgiveness.

To check this possibility, an ingenious solution, soon to be followed by even more ingenious solutions, was devised. Absolution would be given immediately after confession and in advance of the performance of the penance. Again the good news was purchased at the price of some bad news. If such were done, the only warrant for giving absolution at all would be the interior dispositions of the penitent—the quality of sorrow, for example—and not the reform of life which penance was supposed to insure. But then, since the very concept "debt" was removed from the sin-forgiveness life process, it did not matter that its payment was delayed.

In fact it did not matter who paid the debt. Ten years of fasting by one person is the same as one year by ten. Others could pay the debt for you. The living could pay the debt for both the living and the dead, and even the dead, should they have arrived in the afterlife with a surplus of good, could be tapped for the living and the dead. The concepts of remissions, substitutions, and finally indulgences all owe their origin to this fundamental insight as to how in the communion of saints, people help each other towards forgiveness. It is a long way from the prayer of intercession in the early Church, but the idea, *mutatis mutandis*, is the same.

As is well known, this economic model, using the concepts of debt and merit to cancel each other out, had its influence on the Eucharist as well. Once it is established that the "unused" merit of the saints can be tapped via indulgences to erase debt for both the living and the dead, the infinite merit of Christ's sacrifice presents itself as the even more obvious source to tap. And of course the seeds are sown for the bizarre abuses in Eucharistic *praxis* that eventually triggered off the sixteenth century Reformation. The tragedy in all this from a theological perspective is that both the Eucharist and the sacrament of reconciliation were caught in this odd world of economic exchange, and both moved further and further away from the human transformation that is the heart of each.

In its response to the Protestant Reformation, the Catholic Church in the Council of Trent issued fifteen canons on the sacrament of reconciliation, by now firmly called the sacrament of penance. Of prime concern were the following: the existence of penance as a true sacrament instituted by Christ (Canons 1–3); the necessity in God's design of this sacrament (Canons 6–8); the sacramental and juridical role of the priest-confessor (Canons 9–11, 15); and the ingredients essential to the sacrament itself, namely, contrition, confession, absolution, and satisfaction (Canons 4, 5, 12–15).

The Council of Trent ushered in yet another major phase in the history of the sacrament of reconciliation. The form of the sacrament continued to be a private encounter between priest-confessor and penitent, as it had been developed in and inherited from the Celtic Church. It differed, however, in one regard. The spiritual direction context, which gave birth to this private form of the sacrament, yielded over to a different context, more juridical than pastoral in tone. The penitent was to set before the priest an indication of sincere contrition and repentance, the exact number and species of serious sins committed since the last confession, and a determination to amend his or her life. The priest in turn was to judge the sincerity of contrition and repentance, the integral quality of the confession, and the firmness of purpose to amend one's life. If all was in order, the judgment of forgiveness or absolution was passed and an appropriate satisfaction was assigned. If all was not in order, the judgment of forgiveness was withheld until the missing elements were supplied. Satisfaction was still envisioned in terms of prayer and fasting but in fact was usually assigned in terms of a set number of prayers to which indulgences were attached. Penance was popularly imaged as punishment rather than reformation of life.

The Second Vatican Council and the Current *Ordo Poenitentiae*

In the years surrounding the Second Vatican Council, the limitations of this "law court" model for the sacrament began to show themselves, and it became clear that some liturgical therapy was needed if this sacrament was to continue to serve people's true needs. The primary symptom was not, as some have ventured to suggest, a concoction of liturgical experts needing to ply their liturgical trade. The primary symptom surfaced in the lives of the faithful, who suddenly broke familiar patterns of regular, frequent confession and simply stopped coming. While there were some who abandoned more than just this practice of frequent confession and in fact parted company with the Church altogether, for many more this drastic shift in confessional practice was not linked to any other sign of negative feelings towards the Church. It was quite the opposite; confessions declined, and Eucharistic participation increased.

It is not yet clear exactly what the significance of this latter phenomenon really is, and it has received a variety of negative and positive interpretations. It certainly indicates what has been mentioned elsewhere in this work, that the consciousness of sin is changing and that people do not experience any real need for the confessional patterns that were so strong before the council. It seems clear that the substitution of a reconciliation room for the confessional box has not reversed the trend, and it seems to be a sure bet that preconciliar patterns will not return. Perhaps the people are quietly regaining the Eucharist as the primary sacrament of reconciliation, and perhaps the need for an auxiliary ritual primarily focused on sin and forgiveness has passed. But this last possibility is difficult to entertain where the destructive force of sin remains so evident in the world and in human life. More likely if we attend to the patterns of history, the need is there, and the challenge for the Church is to hear the needs of the people of the Church and find new ways to respond to those needs both liturgically and extraliturgically.

The new liturgical rites presented in the revised *Ordo Poenitentiae* are a first attempt to respond to new needs. It is a first attempt, not a final response. Again, if history is any judge of things, it will take a far longer period of time than has elapsed since the Second Vatican Council for an adequate liturgical response to be made. Yet the new rites are a significant advance.

One of the most notable features of the three rituals for the sacrament offered in the *Ordo Poenitentiae* is that all three have the same ritual structure. And it is a liturgical structure. There is a liturgy of the Word, followed by some form of interchange between presider and penitent in which sinfulness is acknowledged and pastoral advice given, followed by absolution which leads into a prayer of thanksgiving. The liturgical nature of the sacrament is most clear in Rite III, common confession and absolution over several penitents together. It is in its entirety a liturgical act. It is somewhat less clear in Rite II, which combines a *common* liturgy of the Word, *individual* confession and absolution, and a *common* thanksgiving. It is least evident in Rite I, which is the form for individual confession and absolution *simpliciter*, and this form oddly enough remains the preferred form for the sacrament. But for all three the structure is the same, and it is a liturgical structure, announcing that the sacrament in whatever form it is enacted is not primarily a juridical act, but is primarily a liturgical act.

As a liturgical act the guiding norm for enacting the sacrament is the proclamation of the Word. This is most especially important for Rite I, where the Word is given as optional. This is not a law court situation, where the priest is to judge the integrity of the confession and the adequacy of the contrition. Priest and penitent both are placed under the Word, and the terms of the exchange ought to resemble a prayerful communal discernment rather than a legal judgment. The ministry of the priest is in all three instances a presidential ministry, that is, a ministry of prayer. The priest is to help the penitent present himself or herself in integral honesty before God, to pray with the penitent for forgiveness, and to proclaim God's forgiveness with effective force.

The pastoral success or inadequacy of these three rituals is reflected on in the commentary attached to the first alternative presented in this volume, and there is no need to repeat that here. Two observations about the current rituals will suffice for the purposes of this historical reflection.

The first concerns not one but two needs which the rituals seek to satisfy. There is on the one hand the personal need for reconciliation which is the traditional point of focus for the sacrament of reconciliation. This is named in the introduction to the rituals in terms of new beginnings and radical conversion. It is here that the personal form of the sacrament is at its best, for it allows the penitent all the time needed to name the sinful situation which is the point of departure and also the time needed to explore together with the confessor the necessary paths forward. Ideally this should not be burdened by a tight schedule or a need to get on to someone else, which is why Rite II, even though it includes private confession, cannot really satisfy this need. But this personal need requires not only a proper amount of time as the ritual is enacted; it could actually involve several enactments of the sacrament over a much longer period of time. A personal need ought to follow a personal timetable and be met in an arena that is totally personal in its contours. The spiritual direction context which gave birth to the private form of the sacrament in the first place probably remains the proper context for this personal need to be met.

In addition to this personal need, however, there is also a communal need which the rituals seek to address. This common need, by the very fact that it is common, does not demand the intensely personal dynamics of the first. It does not require either new beginnings or radical conversion but follows dynamics of a different sort. Its purpose is to celebrate the Church's faith in God's forgiveness of sins in Christ and to keep alive the conviction that forgiveness is readily available in the Church. This is a need on the part of all, to keep the truth of forgiveness in memory so that when it is in fact more personally needed, people will not have forgotten that truth. This faith can and needs to be celebrated as part of the ordinary fare of our liturgical praying, "lest we forget."

There is the personal need and the communal need, and the two are related but quite different. This forms the second observation I want to make. Each of the rituals, regardless of what the introductions may say, imagines sin in exactly the same way. It would be nice to assume that Rite I was for the personal need and Rites II and III for the communal, but this is simply not the case. Rite III would not be so restricted and necessarily tied into an eventual enactment of Rite I were this the case.

Ironically even though three forms are given, because they do imagine sin in the same way, they are essentially the same liturgical ritual after all. If sin is experienced as personal, communal, and social, as the contemporary consciousness seems to indicate it is, it would have to be said that the current rituals leave both the communal and the social unaddressed. The only real question that may be put to each of these rituals is how well it responds to the personal experience of sin and the personal need which that involves. As Denis Woods has pointed out, ritual forms directed primarily if not exclusively toward the reconciliation of individuals cannot be asked to serve the reconciliation of groups. In fact one may question just how successful these rituals may be for achieving reconciliation among persons. It would seem that radically different forms of the sacrament would have to be developed if these other needs for reconciliation, namely, between persons and between groups, are to be served by this reconciling action of the Church.

Thus we stand in the present, still relatively close to the remarkable event of the Second Vatican Council, which stands as a major turning point in the history of all sacramental *praxis*. We also stand at the beginning of a period of transition, which, if the experience and needs of people are seriously attended to, should yield a far more varied future for this sacrament than it has known thus far in its history. We are a long way from the initial insight of "inner transformation" as the primary goal of reconciliation in all of its forms and from the primacy of the Eucharist as the sacrament of this inner transformation, but we are definitely on the trail of recapturing both. The time is ripe for this sacramental tradition to open itself beyond the realm of personal sin and individual absolution to new and broader experiences of sin in the interpersonal, communal, and social realms. Denis Woods' critique still stands. So does the challenge he raises. It can only be hoped that the future holds more promise of success in the broad range of reconciliation than has the past.

A Brief Exploration into the Realm of Reconciliation Among Groups

As this historical chapter comes to a close, the challenge of the reconciliation of groups lingers. It has not directly entered the above reflections, because the history of the sacrament in its narrow sense does not directly invite such reflections. But the history of the sacramental Church in its mission and ministry to reconcile is not completely silent in this regard. The history of the sacrament in its broader sense does have something to say that may help to guide and shape the future. Four pieces of this history can be noted and four actions cited towards this end: prophecy, conciliar action, mediation, and interdict. This historical reflection will end with some brief comments on each.

PROPHECY

Prophecy is usually the action of an individual summoned by God to address God's own Word to an assemblage, be it a community, a group, a church, a nation. It is a forceful summons to conversion, if indeed the behavior within the group cries out for conversion and change. The Old Testament prophets summoned Israel to return to the ways of God. Jesus himself called for repentance and conversion among the peoples. And the Church which he founded has known this prophetic voice in countless men and women who have stood up in the midst of social abuse and violence and neglect and called for action and behavior more in tune with the human dignity and respect which each person demands. Prophecy is the summons of God's Word, and God's Word, as the first step in all sacramental act and process, is an integral part of the sacrament of reconciliation.

CONCILIAR ACTION

The Church itself has not been spared division among its ranks. One need only note the drastic divisions that abound between Eastern and Western Christians and within the West between Protestants of different traditions and Roman Catholics. Recall Denis Woods' wonder why Christians continue to do apart what they could do together.

Efforts to reconcile these groups within the Church have long been the stuff of councils and synods. Some were successful, many were not. Yet the council and the synod remain powerful tools for the reconciliation of groups. Groups must get together to iron out their differences, and they must do so in the context of a larger reality, which may serve to relativize the differences which they hold. Councils and synods are not simply get-togethers. They meet under the sign of the whole, which summons its various parts to harmonious union. The remarkable work of the World Council of Churches is a stunning instance of this move to reconcile groups.

MEDIATION

In addition to conciliar action, a third mechanism which has been employed by the reconciling Church to overcome differences within and among groups is mediation. Someone is appointed to act as arbiter of the differences, usually someone from outside the groups with a position and authority to represent a larger unity. Apostolic visitors to religious communities are but one case in point. The role of the Vatican in intervening in political disputes between nations is another.

INTERDICT

This is action of a different sort. It employs power, and it will only be successful where that power is recognized and respected. It is also vulnerable to being abused, as all power is. Nonetheless, as a last resort when mediation attempts fail, power has been used to force people into changing their ways from alienation and division. Interdict imposes religious sanctions on a group much the same way that excommunication imposes religious sanctions on an individual. It is a most forceful prophetic act, but it appeals to pressure rather than to freedom. This may be its greatest liability. In the long run such pressure is itself divisive and may only serve to hinder, not advance, the reconciliation process.

The current situation in the Church seems to be one of growing consciousness of the variety of human sinfulness affecting human wholeness, human interaction, human social structures, and patterns of human behavior. The challenge of the sacrament of reconciliation and the challenge to the Church's mission and ministry to reconcile and enact Christ's victory over sin, are precisely challenges to meet this growing awareness with responsive action. The alternative futures contained in this volume are but a slight glimpse into the possibilities that are the Church's to meet this complex challenge and to take its noble history of reconciliation firmly into the future.

References

For the history of reconciliation, the works of Palmer and Poschmann remain classic: *Sacraments and Forgiveness* by Paul Palmer [*Sources of Christian Theology, Volume II* (Westminster Md.: Newman, 1959)]; and *Penance and the Anointing of the Sick* by Bernhard Poschmann [trans. F. Courtney (New York: Herder and Herder, 1964)]. More recent works include: *Sign of Reconciliation and Conversion* by Monika Hellwig (Wilmington: Glazier, 1982); *The Sacrament of Repentance and Reconciliation* by Clement Tierney (New York: Costello, 1983); *The Reconciling Church: The Rite of Penance* by James Dallen (New York: Pueblo, 1986); and, from the broader perspective of evolution and change, *The Evolving Church and the Sacrament of Penance* by Ladislas Orsy (Denville, N.J.: Dimension, 1978). A final piece that deserves serious attention is the postsynodal exhortation of Pope John Paul II, *Reconciliatio et Paenitentia,* available in translation from the United States Catholic Conference.

RITUALS

ALTERNATIVE 1:
COMMUNAL CELEBRATION OF THE SACRAMENT OF RECONCILIATION WITH INDIVIDUAL PRESENTATION OF SINS AND INDIVIDUAL ABSOLUTION

Walter H. Cuenin

Introduction

Each of the rituals set forth in this volume arises from two sources: a felt need on the part of the author(s) and the challenges presented above to liturgical praxis by Paul Roy, Denis Woods, and Peter Fink. In the present instance the felt need is mine as an associate pastor of a parish where the concern to bring the reconciliation of Christ to people is more than theoretical.

It seems that a gap has once again grown between the forgiveness and reconciliation of Christ which the sacrament makes available and the ordinary lives of ordinary people. There is much concern rightly voiced over the fact that people are not availing themselves of this sacrament with any regularity. The need is clearly there, in broken lives and broken relationships, and in the frustrations of good people overwhelmed by forces of evil they can scarcely name, much less overcome.

Yet the sacrament seems in so many areas to be falling into disuse. A pastor who has regular contact with the dark side of human life, a dark side that cries out for a simple word of healing and forgiveness and the gracious gift of Christ's reconciliation, cannot help but anguish at the apparent impotence of this once so powerful voice. All of us in the Church need to find a way to make the word of Christ's forgiveness and reconciliation more accessible to the people of the Church. This is the primary hope of this ritual suggestion.

The felt need is given even greater urgency as the observations of Roy, Woods, and Fink are set before us. Five in particular shape this specific ritual suggestion: (a) the need for regular enactment of this sacrament if it is to serve the human growth process that is redemption [Roy and Fink]; (b) the need to rehearse the values of the Gospel in a culture whose own values seem so often to be the Gospel's opposite [Roy and Woods]; (c) the need for visibility and communal support in the process of conversion [Woods and Fink]; (d) the need to respect individuals in all their individuality and to give scope within the rite for this diversity [Roy and Fink]; and (e) the need to listen to the people tell us, their ministers, how best they will be served [my own pastoral sense].

With regard to (a), it seems clear that the private form for the sacrament, regardless of the environmental change from "box" to room, has lost its popularity as a "regular" enactment of this sacrament. People seem to want something less individualistic and isolated as their common fare, probably because of (c). As for (b), the influence of television, the newspapers, film, music, what have you, will be hard to challenge, much less overcome, unless we take active steps to hold before ourselves in a whole variety of ways the values and the truth which we hold as Christian people. The fourth need, (d), is harder to get a hold of, except to say that too narrow a definition of the "way" of reconciliation simply excludes a large number of people whose needs and desires are for a different way. Roy's observation that men and women have different needs in the process of reconciliation touches firmly at the heart of it. Largeness, not narrowness, is needed. Finally, in regard to (e), experience is a good teacher. The ritual presented here is successful. When we have enacted it at my parish, the church is full, and people are delighted with the experience.

A few words might help to locate this ritual suggestion. In the post-Vatican II revisions of the liturgy for reconciliation, three ritual forms are offered. Rite I envisions individual confession and individual absolution. Rite III offers absolution over several penitents together in a ritual form that is totally communal. Rite II presents a hybrid ritual, a common setting and service of the Word followed by individual, private confession and absolution.

Rite I addresses the personal need that is captured in the introduction under the heading of radical conversion and new beginnings. As such it cannot be programmed into the prayer life of the community but is dependent on the needs and condition of the individual involved. Rite III could address the more communal needs and desires of people if it were more readily available, but at present its use is restricted. Moreover, though Rite III has met with success and enthusiasm in those not so frequent instances when it has been employed, there is still some concern to be raised about its sacramental adequacy. It just might be too "general." Finally, Rite II tries to combine both the communal need and the personal need but may be criticized for not really succeeding in either. In many ways it is the least successful of the three.

The alternative ritual offered here represents an organic outgrowth of Rite II. It tries to capture the aim of Rite II while eliminating its principal flaws. This ritual suggestion intends to address the communal need, and it does so with greater success, I think, than Rite III could do. In addition, it does not have the restrictions that are attached to Rite III.

This ritual is intended for a parish community of modest size. It is envisioned as a rite that can be programmed into the community's prayer life, and it might best be enacted during Lent and Advent. Other times are also possible. Its chief purpose is to enact regularly the Church's faith that in Christ sin is overcome. It does not require a radical experience of conversion or new beginnings, and in fact it can allow for a great variety of levels of participation, depending on the needs and desires of the participants. It can thus serve as the ordinary "environment" of reconciliation for the whole community, thereby helping them keep alive the reality of forgiveness and reconciliation in their midst. It may also serve to encourage and guide the more private experience of the sacrament if, and when, the need for such arises.

In many ways this ritual form is more properly named an alternative "present." It is a ritual already in common use, with some variations, in a growing number of local assemblies. It is, as noted above, an evolution from the official Rite II, namely, the celebration of reconciliation in common with individual confession and absolution. This ritual overcomes the principal limitation of the official Rite II, in that it preserves the communal dimension of the sacrament by allowing for individual confession in the common arena. This ritual leads off the selection of alternative futures because, while it is not in itself radically new, it is helping to shape the future of the sacrament in the Roman Catholic community. It is thus a "future" being born.

This ritual, as presented in the main text, requires the ministry of a good number of priests. Some suggestions for an alternative use, which would require only one ordained presbyter, will be offered in an appendix. Because of the number of priests and the fact that many of them will come from other local assemblies and may not therefore be well-known to the assembly gathered, special care must be taken to integrate the visiting priests into the local assembly, while at the same time preserving the peculiar presidency of the assembly that belongs to the local pastor.

RITE OF RECONCILIATION

The numbers in brackets refer to the Roman *Rite of Penance*.

Before the service begins, all the priests except the pastor-presider vest in alb and stole and take their places without ceremonial.

A member of the community introduces visiting priests to the assembly.

Any practical announcements, such as the location of confessors at the time of individual confession, are made prior to the opening of the rite.

Introductory Rites

ENTRANCE

As the presider and assistants enter in procession, the assembly begins its prayer with a song intended to gather all into quiet prayer. One possible musical choice for the entrance song would be a simple *Lord, have mercy* sung repeatedly in mantra style.

GREETING

When the presider arrives at the chair, he greets the assembly. A spontaneous greeting, warmly given and modeled on the ones given in the Roman *Rite of Penance*, would be most effective, for example:

Presider: Let us come with confidence before the throne
        of grace
    to receive God's mercy,
    and we shall find pardon and strength
    in our time of need. [48]

May the grace, mercy, and peace
that is from God in Christ Jesus
be with you all. [cf. 49]

ALL: And also with you.

OPENING PRAYER

The opening prayer should be chosen to reflect the tone that will
run throughout the service, for example:

Presider: My brothers and sisters,
              for the mercy of God and the peace that is from
                  on high,
              let us pray:

              Almighty and merciful God,
              you have brought us together in the name of
                  your Son
              to receive your mercy and grace
              in time of our need.
              Open our eyes to see the evil we have done.
              Touch our hearts and convert us to yourself.

              Where sin has divided and scattered,
              may your love make us one again;
              where sin has brought weakness,
              may your power heal and strengthen;
              where sin has brought death,
              may your Spirit raise us to new life.

              Give us a new heart to love you,
              so that our lives may reflect the image of
                  your Son.

              May the world see the glory of Christ
              revealed in your Church
              and come to know
              that he is the One whom you have sent,
              Jesus Christ, your Son, our Lord.

All: Amen.

Liturgy of the Word

READING: 1 John 1:5–2:12

RESPONSE

A meditative psalm or song will allow the word that has been proclaimed to take root in the assembly.

HOMILY

The function of the homily in this ritual is to lead the assembly to see their sins in the light of the word and to confess them with sorrow in order to receive Christ's forgiveness and reconciliation. It is *not* an examination of conscience. The homily should lead naturally into a period of silent reflection to prepare for the enactment of the sacramental rite.

SILENT EXAMINATION OF THE HEART

Rite of Reconciliation

CONFESSION OF SIN

Presider: My brothers and sisters in Christ:
let us enter now into a prayer
of repentance and reconciliation.
We seek together to be purified
of all illusions and false gods,
of all that is sin within us.
We seek the gentle prodding of our God
to give our lives the shape of Christ's own life,
and to draw us more deeply into the promised
      kingdom.

We have examined our lives.
We have seen where the weakness of our faith,
where the failure of our hope,
where the absence of our love,
have been the source of harm to others or
      ourselves.
May we now acknowledge our sin and our
      sorrow
before God and before this assembly
that the healing power and mercy of our God
may touch us once again.

All: I confess to almighty God . . .

Presider: Lord, have mercy!

All: Lord, have mercy!

Presider: Christ, have mercy!

All: Christ, have mercy!

Presider: Lord, have mercy!

All: Lord, have mercy!

Presider: (with hands extended over the assembly)

God the Father of mercies,
through the death and resurrection of your Son,
you have reconciled the world to yourself
and sent the Holy Spirit among us
for the forgiveness of sins.
Through the ministry of the Church
grant us all pardon and peace.
We ask this through Christ, our Lord. [cf. 55]

All: Amen.

Presider: If you wish now to be signed with the
            forgiveness of God,
spoken in the sacrament of the Church,
please come forward.
Acknowledge your sin and your sorrow,
and open your heart to the healing power of
            God.

The priests go to various assigned places in the assembly. All the priests, with the exception of the pastor, receive the confessions and grant absolution. The pastor remains standing in front of the assembly for the laying on of hands following absolution.

As the penitents approach, the priests may welcome them and, in order to establish a more personal contact, may grasp their hands.

Priest: Do you acknowledge that you are a sinner
            before God?

Penitent: I do.

Priest: And are you sorry for all your sins?

Penitent: I am, and especially for . . .

(Here the penitent mentions one or two sins which he/she most needs to present to God for forgiveness).

ABSOLUTION

Priest: In the love of Christ
I absolve you from your sins,
in the name of the Father, and of the Son +,
and of the Holy Spirit. [cf. 55]

Penitent: Amen.

After receiving absolution, each penitent approaches the pastor for the laying on of hands and/or a greeting of peace and then returns to his/her place in the assembly.

PRAYER OF BLESSING AND THANKSGIVING

Presider: Almighty and merciful God,
how wonderfully you created us,
and still more wonderfully remade us.
You do not abandon sinners
but seek us out with a father's love.
You sent your Son into the world
to destroy sin and death by his passion,
and to restore life and joy by his resurrection.

You sent your Holy Spirit into our hearts
to make us your sons and daughters
and heirs to your blessed kingdom.
By this same Spirit, O God,
continue to be with us.

Set us free from all slavery to sin
and transform us ever more closely
into the likeness of your beloved Son.

We thank you for the wonders of your mercy,
and with heart and hand and voice
we join the whole Church
in a new song of praise:
glory to you,
through Christ,
in the Holy Spirit,
now and forever. [cf. 57]

All: Amen.

The assembly sings a song of praise and thanksgiving.

Concluding Rite

Presider:	And now, my brothers and sisters, let us call upon our God in prayer in the words which Jesus gave us:
All:	Our Father . . . . But deliver us from evil. For the kingdom . . . forever and ever. Amen.
Presider:	As we have been reconciled with our God, with each other, and with the Church, may Christ's peace reign always in our hearts.
All:	Amen.
Presider:	May the peace of the Lord be with you.
All:	And also with you.
Presider:	Let us greet each other now in peace.

The service concludes with a festive hymn. An invitation to a social gathering may follow.

Commentary: Content

As is evident, the ritual presented here draws heavily on the official texts of the *Rite of Penance* in current use in the Roman Catholic Church.

ENTRANCE

A service of reconciliation is, by its very nature, a quiet service, and it would not be well served by an elaborate entrance procession. Placing the assistant presbyters in the assembly from the beginning, prior to the procession, both simplifies the entrance rite and highlights the fact that they too are sinners in need of reconciliation, and not simply the "givers" of absolution for others.

LITURGY OF THE WORD

While the Liturgy of the Word might well be structured in the customary manner, with two or even three readings, the nature of this service as a time to dwell in reflective quiet with one's own sinfulness and God's forgiveness suggests the appropriateness of a more streamlined format, distinct from that of the Sunday Eucharist. The choice of a single reading, a meditative song, and a brief homily, as proposed here, also serves to focus attention on the main purpose of the service, namely, to help people present themselves honestly and humbly before our forgiving and reconciling God.

PRAYER FOR FORGIVENESS/DECLARATION OF ABSOLUTION

The prayer for forgiveness and the declaration of absolution that now appear in the official texts combine two traditions: the imprecatory form common in the East and the declaratory form in use in the West since the twelfth century. Many have noted the awkwardness of this combination. The above ritual separates the two traditions, employing the first as a communal prayer in response to the confession of sinfulness and the second in the individual setting in response to the individual's presentation of sin. This division seems to make more ritual sense.

CONFESSION OF SIN

The presentation of sinfulness by individuals is not envisioned here in the strict terms of juridical integrity. Rather, integrity is seen to be the quality of one's honesty before God, not of itself requiring the classical "number and species." One should assume that a person coming before God in the sacrament is honestly seeking God's healing power and not "trying to hold something back." Needless to say, there is no magic here. People effectively receive God's forgiveness to the extent that they are honestly open to doing so.

PRAYER OF BLESSING AND THANKSGIVING

The prayer of thanksgiving that is prayed after all have been absolved is offered as a standard blessing prayer. It could easily begin with the classic dialogue for such prayers. While not a great deal is made of this point here, it is good to reinstate the blessing prayer as an integral part of all of our sacramental actions. Such is the intent here. The blessing prayer remains the primary catechetical and mystagogical element in the ritual. It names the "deeds of God" which we remember and because of which we hope for God's action once again. Inclusion of such a prayer in the rite establishes this sacrament too as anamnesis.

Commentary: Theological Principles

Five points in the introduction, four from the essays which form the earlier part of this volume, were given as needs to which this ritual hopes to respond. I would like here to add some further reflections on the rite in light of these various essays. Several areas have been noted that are impacting upon the sacrament of reconciliation, namely, the changing concept of sin, the power of symbols, and the role of the assembly in all liturgical celebrations. These theological principles are clearly operative in this suggested form of reconciliation.

New Understanding of Sin

It seems that the understanding of sin as an isolated act or personal offense against God that requires apology is giving way to a more inclusive and dynamic understanding. Sin is understood as a manifestation of sinfulness. It is seen more and more as a pattern of life in which the person brings evil to expression by individual choices. It is not something that sets the few apart from the many, the good and the bad as it were. Sin is a condition that is shared by all, a bond of solidarity that links all human beings together in the evil that overpowers the world. It is as sinners that the entire community assembles before the love and mercy of God.

This communal form of penance is clearly suited to respecting and developing this common notion of human sinfulness. The ritual does indeed allow for individual confession of sins, but it stipulates that this be done publicly and in the context of a community action. The ritual sees confession of sins in a way different from that envisioned by the post-Tridentine Church. Confession is not made so that the priest as judge can have the full picture of the individual's life. Rather, it is to offer the individual the opportunity to manifest that he or she is a particular sinner in need of God's particular grace and reconciliation. There is deliberately little opportunity given for priests to speak at length with the penitents. Such individual attention is more proper to the individual form of the sacrament. Presumably, in this common form, the Word proclaimed, and specifically the homily, provide the proper address. In this common form the specifics of each individual's sins are less important than the public gesture which indicates (*signifies*) solidarity with others in being sinner and solidarity with others in the need for mercy and reconciliation.

The Power of Symbols

One of the key elements in contemporary sacramental theory is the fact that sacraments "work" as they signify. The power of the sacrament is to effect an encounter with Christ, and this power lies in its ability to signify such an encounter. This is the prime reason why a public dialogue of penitent with priest is advised. The sacrament's power is for the whole assembly and not just for the individual penitent.

As noted earlier, the official Rite II is a hybrid. It represents a simple inclusion of the post-Tridentine private confession within, yet apart from, a communal celebration. Such a ritual is puzzling at best. In the ritual development of Rite II proposed here, with the confession and proclamation of reconciliation taking place in the midst of the assembly itself, the mode of effectiveness of this sacrament is altered. Signification is expanded. Not only is the power of the sacrament in the word of forgiveness spoken by the priest in the encounter between priest and penitent; the very visibility of the encounter to others contributes to its power. Signification is full, not narrow and restricted.

The symbolic activity of all going to confess and being absolved in full visibility of each other in the assembly shapes the communal imagination. It helps all experience their common bond in sin and their common strength in the reconciliation of Christ. A strong assessment of the people who have celebrated a rite of this kind is that the experience of the entire community going through this together is precisely what makes their experience of reconciliation in Christ so powerful.

THE ROLE OF THE COMMUNITY

Paul stresses the role of the community in the act of reconciliation when he says, "So we are ambassadors for Christ; it is as though God were appealing through us, and the appeal that we make in Christ's name is this: be reconciled to God" (2 Cor 5:20). The early Church knew and expressed the truth of this ministry of all in the value it placed on intercession for sinners. Appeal and intercession are two crucial ministries of the assembly to penitents.

The form of the sacrament presented here changes the nature of the confession of sins. A private confession made publicly is no longer private. Nor, in principle, need it be. The Constitution on the Sacred Liturgy challenged the notion of a private sacrament, urging that "whenever rites, according to their specific nature, make provision for communal celebration involving the presence and active participation of the faithful, this way of celebrating them is to be preferred, as far as possible, to a celebration that is individual and quasi-private" (CSL 27). While the specific nature of the sacrament when it responds to intense personal needs may well demand a private arena for its success, the common need certainly calls for common, public action.

This is not to say that this form of penance removes the need for individuals to experience a more personal and private form of the sacrament. Quite the contrary. It is, in fact, the experience of many that a common ritual experience leads them to seek, at a later date, a longer, more in-depth celebration of reconciliation in the private forum. The communal service can serve to free people from fear and childish understandings of sin so as to empower them to seek further reconciliation. It may well be the experience of the Church in the future that these communal forms of the sacrament will serve to enrich and encourage the more individual ones. If nothing else it will keep us from forgetting that such reconciliation is possible within the Church, an amnesia that is quite possible as the frequency of private, individual confession diminishes.

Appendix

As mentioned in the introduction, the ritual of reconciliation given here is in many ways an "alternative present" rather than an "alternative future." It represents a slight evolution from the official Rite II that is now offered to the Church. Yet it is precisely in this that the power of this ritual is found. Since it is basically an officially approved ritual, it is in fact widely in use in some form or other and is even now serving to shape the consciousness of the Church in regard to the sacrament. Again the phrase, a "future being born."

Yet perhaps further evolution can be envisioned. The official Rite II, and indeed the ritual form presented above, require the priest to receive the confession and to offer absolution individually. Yet, where this ritual form has been employed, two things have come to surface which may give an even more radically different shape to the sacrament in the future. The first concerns the needs of the people and the second the availability of adequate numbers of priests to enact the rite.

In regard to the first, there are indications that some people do not experience the need to express their sins to the priest in order to find reconciliation. Confessing privately to the Lord and going up for the pastor's embrace of peace satisfies their need for reconciliation. In some cases the confession and exploration of life is done with someone else, such as a retreat director, counselor, or friend. What is sought from the Church is not a repeat performance but a confirmation of what has happened. While it is probably too early to judge this phenomenon, it does seem to be an area where a significant evolution of the sacrament is occurring.

The second point, namely, the difficulty in gathering adequate numbers of priests for the service, raises an even more serious and challenging issue for the future. As the number of ordained priests continues to decline, it must be asked if this communal rite could be so adapted as to allow the individual expression of sinfulness, where desired, to be given to someone other than the ordained priest, with the priest-pastor giving individual absolution with a laying on of hands, a prayer, and an embrace. In other words the question arises whether there could be established in each local assembly a new lay ministry where men and women are selected and trained as ministers of reconciliation. This too would respond to Paul Roy's challenge.

The advantage of such an evolution would be two-fold. Outsiders would not have to be imported for this special event, and the absolution prayer would regain its stature as a prayer of invocation prayed by the presider of the assembly. Moreover, it would help us discover again that, while it is important for penitents to present themselves in human integrity to the Lord, the person who proclaims the consecratory prayer of absolution need not be the same as the one who receives the presentation of sins. Were such a lay ministry developed within local assemblies, it would allow the members of the assembly to retain the opportunity for the individual expression of sinfulness, something needed for people to deal personally with evil in their lives and thus preserve this important ritual dimension. This might be a more helpful direction to move in than the more obvious resort to Rite III, which does not allow individual expression of sinfulness at all.

In addition to the question of practicality, it must be asked what sense can be made of "importing" priests into an assembly. If confession of sin is to be a part of the community's ritual of reconciliation, we must seriously wonder whether the confession can be made to someone who is not part of the community. Reconciliation is not only private and personal; it is public and communitarian. The ministers of reconciliation, therefore, need to be connected with the community and in a deeper sense *must* be members of the community in which the sacrament is celebrated.

In a strange twist the official Rite II of the sacrament, most inadequate of the three in its official garb, has helped hasten other possibilities for structuring this sacrament. The requirement of individual confession in some form or other coupled with the difficulty of bringing many priests together have created a tension that seeks resolution. As Rite II continues to evolve, the need to maintain confession within a communal context will challenge the Church to explore new alternatives.

What is offered here is a mild alternative. It is oriented to the future, yet it is firmly rooted in the tradition of the Church. The value of dealing personally with one's sinfulness is maintained. The role of the priest as the one who announces and proclaims Christ's forgiveness is likewise preserved. What differs from the preconciliar practice is the mode in which the confession of sins is made. The classical theology only required that all serious sin be confessed to the priest in so far as it was possible. Psychological and moral impossibility always excused from this requirement. Perhaps, as the availability of priests becomes less and the communal value of a service such as presented here gains currency, this time-honored insight will find a new home.

Rite II is a new ritual already in the process of being renewed. Its alternative future is contained in the present. The process of evolution is clearly under way, from an official ritual of the Church to a possible future ritual, the shape of which has many exciting possibilities. Modest though it be, the ritual presented here moves into that future.

ALTERNATIVE 2:
LITURGY OF RECONCILIATION WHERE UNORDAINED MINISTERS RECEIVE THE CONFESSION OF SIN, PRAY FOR FORGIVENESS AND RECONCILIATION, AND TOGETHER PRESENT THIS FOR CONFIRMATION AND COMPLETION IN THE LITURGICAL ASSEMBLY

Peter E. Fink, S.J.

Introduction

This second ritual, like the first, arises both from a felt need and from several challenges presented in the essays that precede. In this case the felt need comes from a dilemma in which my students not infrequently find themselves. Any dilemma for one's students is a dilemma for the teacher as well. For my students the dilemma most often presents itself when they are serving as chaplains in hospitals. Now and again patients ask them to hear their confessions. The dilemma: what to do?

The simple answer, of course, is for them to say, "I am not a priest," and then arrange for a priest, if possible, to come and visit the patient. But I pose a question to them in return, like the good Jesuit I am, and in so doing increase, rather than dispel, their dilemma. "What if the person should die that night, before you have had a chance to contact a priest? Clearly the patient has taken you to be in some way a representative of the Church and a representative of Christ, or he or she would not have asked you in the first place. And if you say simply no, that rejection may well be the last word the patient hears from you, and therefore from the Church, and the patient will die without the comfort Christ wishes us to bring. Surely there is something you can do to respond pastorally, and sacramentally, to the patient's request." And surely there is.

This kind of dilemma, in fact, goes beyond my students in the divinity school, most of whom are not ordained priests, though many eventually will be. It includes women religious, men religious who are not priests, and an increasing number of lay people who are more and more being engaged in ministries such as spiritual direction, retreat direction, and hospital chaplaincy. In such positions they find people presenting to them classic "confessional" material for discussion and unraveling, or simply for prayer. They are not asked to hear anyone's confession; they discover that that is in fact what they are doing. And they discover even more that in those instances they become much more than a "willing ear" and a kindly presence with some helpful advice. Both penitent and minister find that the interchange produces a healing and a sense of reconciliation and forgiveness that is very much the stuff of the sacrament.

Where this kind of thing happens, the question of sacramental reconciliation becomes problematic. On the one hand, it seems improper, and disrespectful of the manifest power of God present in the event, to treat the occurrence as if it had no sacramental significance at all and to ask the penitent to "go through it all again" with an ordained priest. On the other hand, it seems equally improper to equate this event *simpliciter* with the sacrament of the Church. For reasons of faith, tradition, and discipline, the Church requires an ordained priest to proclaim the absolution of sin.

So the question remains for my students, for the teacher, and for the growing army of ministers who are not priests: what to do, and how to understand the proper sacramental response to these situations? Clearly the "all-or-nothing" option, the valid-invalid option, is not adequate to resolve the issue.

In addition to this dilemma, which, while not without precedent, is a relatively new phenomenon in the contemporary Church, several issues raised in this volume encourage even more the development of a ritual response such as is presented here. Paul Roy's citations from Lillian Rubin have haunted me since I read them, particularly in light of another reality that has surfaced of late in my experience. An increasing number of women, no doubt influenced in part by the Church's position on the ordination of women, have voiced a difficulty they have in finding reconciliation through the ministry of a male priest. In a service such as the one which Walter Cuenin offers as Alternative 1, they requested that some women be available, not for absolution, but at least for a prayer and a blessing. During the service, many of the women were in fact comfortable in seeking reconciliation from the priests in the standard sacramental form. But some of them, and what is even more interesting, some of the men also, preferred the ministry of the women to that of the men.

Paul Roy's challenge that men and women have different needs in general when it comes to reconciliation is enough to urge some way, even if that way is not, as it seems for the present, ordination, to enlist the aid of women along side of men in the ministry of reconciliation. Some men and some women will be most helped toward reconciliation by a man, and others by a woman. And it is the reconciliation of Christ, not the particular sex of the particular minister, that is, finally, the issue. But this is in general. It would seem to me to be even more urgent when, for reasons which may be good or bad, healthy or unhealthy, permanent or relatively transient, the gender of the minister becomes a positive obstacle to reconciliation. We must remember that the truth of reconciliation is that, in Christ, God accepts us *as we are.* The burden must always fall on the Church, which is mandated to reconcile, to enlist ministers to carry out that mandate, even if it must break familiar patterns and radically expand the way it imagines the reconciliation ministry. As it is with baptism, that when a man or a woman baptizes, it is Christ who baptizes, so it is, we must presume, with reconciliation also.

The second point from the preceding essays that encourages this ritual suggestion is the recognition that the process of reconciliation is a process with both psychological and spiritual dimensions to it. With Paul Roy we can call it growing up and see the process in terms of therapy. Theologically we can call it redemption and see it in terms of conversion and spiritual direction. In either case, if the preferred arena for the private form of the sacrament is, as I think it is, spiritual direction, then we have to include in the sacramental ministry all those men and women who are in fact doing spiritual direction.

A third issue is only implicit in what has gone before. I have said that the personal and communal needs for reconciliation ought not be confused or conflated. They are two distinct needs that require their own proper dynamics, timetable, and arena. They ought not be conflated, but they ought to be related. The private enactment of the sacrament can never be totally private, isolated from any and all community reference. Why the requirement of an ordained priest in the first place if not to represent and embody the ecclesial dimension of this act even in its most private form?

I personally find it odd that one restriction attending the current use of Rite III, "general absolution," is that the recipients are then asked to bring this to the private arena within a reasonable amount of time. I am convinced that the opposite is in fact the case. Recipients of forgiveness in the private arena need to come to the common arena if forgiveness is to be likewise reconciliation. The community needs them to come if it is to have cause to celebrate a more than theoretical faith. We need to know that forgiveness does happen in order to continue to believe that it may happen again.

Vatican II gave priority to the communal form of the celebration of sacraments precisely because the sacraments help the whole Church to grow. The conviction here is that the private form does need its own space and time but that it cannot be seen as complete until it is brought to the communal arena of worship. The ritual presented here offers one model of that "bringing to completion."

Finally there is the point mentioned by Walter Cuenin in his comments on Alternative 1 and its possible evolution in the future. With the shortage of priests mounting, Cuenin suggested establishing a lay ministry of reconciliation within local Church communities. With proper adaptation, this ritual could serve that evolution in a way different from Cuenin's own. I could imagine a week, or even a month, devoted to reconciliation in a local Church community where many ministers, in homes, in confessional rooms, or wherever, employ the first part of the ritual presented here according to the dynamics required of each individual penitent, with the whole community gathering at the end of that time for a celebration of part two to complete and confirm in common assembly what has happened in the many private arenas throughout the parish.

This, then, is the rationale for the two parts of the ritual. The first is intended to serve the individual interchange which may take place with a retreat director, a spiritual director, or a hospital chaplain. The second, which is viewed as complementary to and continuous with the first, brings the sacramental act into the liturgical assembly for confirmation and completion.

Essential to both parts is this connection between them. They are viewed together as a single sacramental act occurring in two phases. It is essential that the second be seen as confirming and completing the first.

RITE OF RECONCILIATION

Part I: Private Reconciliation

What is offered here may serve as a resource and guide to the minister in order that the ingredients essential to reconciliation be observed. However, because of the intensely personal nature of the exchange between penitent and minister in the private arena of spiritual direction, retreat direction, or hospital visitation, rigid adherence to a given ritual structure would be inappropriate. Therefore, the parts of the suggested ritual need not follow as they are given here, particularly in a spontaneous encounter.

The numbers in brackets refer to the text of the Roman *Rite of Penance*.

GREETING

Minister: My brother (sister),
you have come before me,
a fellow member of the Church,
to acknowledge your sinfulness
and to explore the path of reconciliation.
I am humbled and honored,
and I pray that God's loving Spirit
give me wisdom and compassion to serve you
        well.
May the peace of Christ be in your heart.

Penitent: Amen.

CELEBRATION OF THE WORD OF GOD

The Word of God may be read or incorporated into an informal address similar to this example:

Minister: My brother (or sister),
as you come before God to present your sins
in faith and in hope,
remember that our God is not a harsh,
        demanding God.
Our God is gentle, and merciful, and
        compassionate.
Remember the words of the prophet Isaiah.
To you our God says:

> "You are precious in my eyes,
> and honored, and I love you" (Isa 43:4).

> To you our God proclaims,
> "Even if a mother should forget the child she has
>   nursed,
> I will never forget you" (Isa 49:15).

> Approach our God now in confidence and in
>   trust.

INTERCHANGE BETWEEN PENITENT AND MINISTER

By its very nature, this interchange between penitent and minister does not have any ritual structure. For a description of its tasks and essential content, see commentary, p. 118.

PRAYERS OF REPENTANCE AND FORGIVENESS

Minister: May I ask you now to come before the Lord
and speak in prayer your sorrow and repentance.

The penitent may respond in his/her own words or as follows:

Penitent: My God,
I am sorry for my sins with all my heart.
In choosing to do wrong
and failing to do good
I have sinned against you
whom I should love above all else.
I firmly intend, with your help,
to do penance,
to sin no more,
and to avoid whatever leads me to sin. [cf. 45]

The minister may lay hands on the penitent's head while saying the following prayer:

Minister: Our savior, Jesus Christ,
suffered and died for us.
In his name I pray upon you God's pardon and
peace.

Penitent: Amen.

CONCLUDING PRAYERS

Minister: As a prayer of repentance and of praise,
let us pray together as Jesus has taught us to
pray:

Both: Our Father . . . . But deliver us from evil.
For the kingdom . . . forever. Amen.

Minister: May the Lord continue to guide your heart
in the way of his love.
May the Lord give you peace
now and for all days to come.

Penitent: Amen.

The minister may add in these or similar words:

Minister: God has in Christ forgiven your sins
and reconciled you.
In time, let us come before the Church,
in the midst of our brothers and sisters,
to confirm and complete what is begun this day
for our own good and the good of all.

Go now in peace.

Penitent: May God be praised, now and forever. Amen.

Part II: Completion in Liturgical Assembly

Part II of the rite as printed here serves as the communal completion of the sacramental process of forgiveness and reconciliation begun in the meeting between individual penitents and ministers of reconciliation either in a group setting, such as a retreat, or at various times throughout the previous week, such as spiritual direction sessions. In either case, penitents and ministers come together at an appropriate time to carry out the completion of the rite of penance as it is given below. If Part I has involved only a single penitent, as it might in the course of a hospital visit, then Part II may be adapted accordingly. In such a case, the adaptation should preserve the understanding that Part II is the completion of a sacramental process already begun in the earlier encounter between penitent and minister.

In this ritual, the term *minister* refers to one of the people who has served as minister of reconciliation in Part I of the rite. This minister may or may not be ordained, but he/she is other than the presider. He/she is chosen as spokesperson for the team of ministers. *Presider*, on the other hand, refers to the priest-presider of the liturgical action.

ENTRANCE AND INTRODUCTORY RITE

Since this part of the liturgy of reconciliation is envisioned as the completion of a sacramental process already begun, it is more festive in character than a liturgy that would have to bring people to sorrow and repentance. Therefore a song of joy and gratitude would be an appropriate opening hymn.

All of the ministers of reconciliation who have taken part in Part I of the rite should enter and take their places with the presider.

GREETING

Presider: My sisters and brothers,
                  may the peace of the Lord, Jesus Christ
                  be with you all.

All: And also with you.

GLORY TO GOD

Presider: Though we have sinned, we do not lose heart,
                  for we have Jesus Christ to plead for us
                  with the Father.
                  He is the Holy One,
                  the atonement for our sins,
                  and for all the sins of the world.

                  Let us acclaim the glory of our God:

All sing: Glory to God in the highest . . . .

OPENING PRAYER

Presider: Let us pray:

                  Lord, our God,
                  you are kind and merciful to sinners,
                  and you bless our desire
                  to amend and renew our life.

                  We confess our sins in the midst of your Church,
                  and firmly resolve to change our lives.

                  Help us to complete this sacrament of your
                      mercy
                  so that, with the help of your guiding Spirit,
                  we may reform our lives,
                  give witness to your reconciliation,

and receive at last from you
the gift of everlasting joy.
We ask this through Christ, our Lord.

All: Amen.

Liturgy of the Word

READING: 2 Cor 5:16-21

RESPONSORIAL PSALM: Ps 23

R̷. His goodness shall follow me always,
all the days of my life.

GOSPEL ACCLAMATION: Ps 51:12

Alleluia . . .
Create in me a clean heart,
and renew within me an upright spirit.
Alleluia . . . .

GOSPEL: John 21:4-17

HOMILY

Rite for the Confirmation and Completion of Reconciliation

Minister: Let those who would complete their
reconciliation
with God and with the Church
please come forward.

If the number of penitents is large, they may stand in their places;
if sufficiently small, they may come forward to a previously desig-
nated place before the presider. If appropriate, their names may be
called.

One of the ministers of reconciliation presents the penitents to the
presider in the name of all.

Minister: Father *N.*,
and all members of the assembly here present,
we present these men and women to you
that you may confirm the forgiveness of God
which is theirs
and complete their reconciliation with the
Church.

Presider: Do you judge that it is right for us to do so?

Minister: They have acknowledged their sin before us,
have been touched by the healing power of God,
and have earnestly begun on the path of
repentance and reconciliation.
We judge that it is right and just.

Presider: The Lord continues to do wonderful things
among us.
Through the ministry of the Church
may God bring to completion what God has
begun.

All: Thanks be to God.

A joyful song of God's graciousness may be sung.

INSTRUCTION TO THE PENITENTS

Presider: My brothers and sisters in Christ.
You have confessed your sins before the Lord
in the presence of these ministers.
With their aid you have given new shape to
your lives,
that you may be holy, even as the Lord is holy.

Through their compassion you have known
the compassion of our God;
in their forgiveness you have seen and tasted
the forgiveness won for us by Jesus Christ.
Always remember the words of Paul proclaimed
this day,
that you must give to others
what has been given to you.

God has entrusted to us this message of
reconciliation,
that through us all men and women
may be reconciled to God.
As we rejoice with you this day,
and proclaim the forgiveness and reconciliation
of God,
so likewise we commission you:
live a life worthy of the calling you have
received,

be kind and compassionate and forgiving to all,
that in you God may be glorified,
and through you Christ's work of redemption
    carried on.

DECLARATION OF PENITENTS' INTENT

Presider: My sisters and brothers,
before you come forward for the laying on of
    hands
and the prayer of absolution,
I ask you to declare before God and before this
    assembly
your sorrow, your true repentance,
and your firm resolve to sin no more.
Have you confessed your sins before the Lord
in full honesty and integrity,
and with deep sorrow of heart?

Penitents: We have.

Presider: Are you determined with the help of God's grace
to shun the ways of sin,
and to follow the gracious way of Jesus Christ?

Penitents: We are.

Presider: As the Lord has forgiven you,
will you strive to forgive and love
all your sisters and brothers?

Penitents: We will.

Presider: May I ask you then to acknowledge your sin
    and your sorrow
before the Lord and this assembly
that we may be with you in prayer
and reconcile you in love.

Penitents: I confess to almighty God . . . .

PRAYER FOR FORGIVENESS AND ABSOLUTION

Presider: My brothers and sisters,
do you earnestly desire the forgiveness of God
and reconciliation with the Church
through the ministry of our prayer
and the proclamation of absolution?

Penitents: We do.

Presider: (extending his hands over the penitents)

God the Father does not wish the sinner to die
but to turn back and live.
God loved us first and sent the only Son into the
    world to be its Savior.
May God show you merciful love and give you
    peace.

Penitents: Amen.

Presider: Our Lord Jesus Christ was given up to death
    for our sins,
and rose again for our justification.
He sent the Holy Spirit on his apostles
and gave them the power to forgive sins.
Through the ministry entrusted to me
may he deliver you from evil
and fill you with his Holy Spirit.

Penitents: Amen.

Presider: The Spirit, the Comforter, was given to us for
    the forgiveness of sins.
In the Spirit we approach the Father.
May the Spirit cleanse your hearts and clothe you in
    glory,
so that you may proclaim the mighty acts of
    God
who has called you out of darkness into the
    splendor of divine light.

Penitents: Amen.

Each penitent now comes forward for the laying on of hands and
the proclamation of absolution. The presider places his right hand
on the penitent's head or shoulder while saying:

Presider: I absolve you from your sins,
and reconcile you to God and to the Church,
in the name of the Father, and of the Son +,
and of the Holy Spirit.

Penitent: Amen.

The penitent returns to his/her place.

Concluding Rites

Presider: My sisters and brothers,
let us join now in prayer to the Father
as Jesus has taught us to pray:

All: Our Father . . . But deliver us from evil
For the kingdom . . . forever and ever. Amen.

Presider: And may the peace of the Lord be with you all.

All: And also with you.

Presider: As a sign of our reconciliation,
let us greet each other in peace.

When the greeting of peace has been completed:

Presider: May the Lord be with you.

All: And also with you.

Presider: Let us pray.
God and Father of us all,
you have forgiven our sins
and sent us your peace.
Help us to forgive each other
and to work together to establish
a reign of peace in the world.
We ask this through Christ, our Lord [cf. 211].

All: Amen.

Presider: Go in peace,
and proclaim to the world
the wonderful works of God
who has brought salvation to us all.

All: Thanks be to God.

A song of joy concludes the service.

Commentary: Content

The first part of the ritual given here is modeled after Rite I of the sacrament as given in the *Rite of Penance*, with adjustments made to link it with the second part.

Whether this ministry is done by a priest or lay minister, the same dynamic is required, and the same skills must be employed. If the truth be told, it would probably make very little existential difference to the penitent whether the minister was a priest who said, "I absolve you," or a lay minister whose words were in the more imprecatory form. The fact that many educated Catholics wonder about the need for the former when the latter has taken place indicates that the issue is not well resolved on the existential level. Nor is it well resolved when only minister and penitent are taken into account, and when the entire assembly gathered is left out of the picture. Sacraments are for the whole Church and not just for a few. Hopefully, the ritual itself will educate people to an awareness that the existential, the ecclesial, and the symbolic dimension are all necessarily related.

Two pieces of this first part call for special notice, the celebration of the Word and the interchange between penitent and minister. The Roman Rite of Reconciliation of Individual Penitents (Rite I) calls for an optional reading from the Word of God. It is unfortunate that the rite does not urge this more strongly. It is the proclamation of the Word that alters radically the nature of the interchange between penitent and minister, changing it from self-accusation before a judge to self-presentation to a loving and forgiving God. The use of Scripture is urged strongly here, though an informality proper to the intimacy of the one-on-one interchange is called for. An example of this informality is given in the rite.

As for the interchange between penitent and minister, by its very nature it does not have any strict ritual structure. It does have several tasks which the minister is asked to fulfill on the part of the penitent. Chief among them is assistance so that the penitent may present himself/herself in full honesty, integrity, and authenticity before the Lord. For this the minister must be most respectful of the penitent and consider it his/her utmost aim to embody the welcome, understanding and compassion of God.

Other goals of this interchange include: counsel and guidance toward a reformation of life, particularly in regard to the matter under discussion, help in selecting some prayer or action which would serve to begin the amendment process (i.e., penance), assistance where necessary toward the proper affections of sorrow and repentance. This last involves taking the material presented with utter seriousness as sin and not trying to "psychologize" the matter away.

The proclamation in the sacrament is always that God loves us, even in the face of our sinfulness, and that God in his gracious mercy takes our sin and transforms it into non-sin. It is important that the penitent hear God's love in the face of sin and not simply find help to excuse the sin away.

The second part of the ritual is modeled on the rituals of ordination. Another liturgical tradition, that of "supplying the ceremonies" for a baptism performed in emergency circumstances was also considered, but judged finally not to yield as hopeful a path to follow. In some ways this rite echoes an "order of penitents" for which there is ample precedent in the history of the Church. It is solemn in tone. The intent is to highlight the public nature of reconciliation and the public ministry that those who are reconciled perform for the Church community. To paraphrase Paul, how shall we know sin is forgiven if no one ever tells us it is so?

Commentary: Theological Principles

The rite presented here calls for the employment of lay ministers for the compassionate reception of the penitent's sin, while at the same time reserving the full proclamation of absolution and reconciliation to the ordained president of the liturgical assembly. It recognizes the lay ministers and the ministry they perform as an integral part of the sacramental action, yet it sees that ministry as ordered to completion by a complementary act of the Church in assembly. This employment of lay ministers in the act of reconciliation is not without precedent in the Church. For example, in the Middle Ages soldiers confessed to one another. Nor is the extension of sacramental activity beyond the currently accepted norm unheard of. It must be recalled that in its early stages of development, the practice of private confession as it had evolved in the Celtic Church was somewhat *ex lex*, a fact noted with some force at the Third Synod of Toledo in 589 and still a source of contention at the time of the ninth-century reform synods, most especially the Synod of Chalon in 813.

At any rate the warrant for suggesting this ritual at this point in the Church's life is not based so much on historical precedent as it is in the present, on developments in sacramental understanding that have come from Vatican II and the increased awareness of the reconciliation process that has come from the human sciences. The Constitution on the Sacred Liturgy recognized that all sacraments are liturgical actions and that therefore they are always, first and foremost, actions of the Church in assembly. Any form of any sacrament will be properly understood only if its normative enactment by the assembled Church is taken into account (CSL 26, 27).

This is true even where, for practical, pastoral, or other reasons, the full assembly is present only symbolically in the person and ministry of the ordained priest. In all liturgical actions it is the full assembly of the Church hierarchically gathered that constitutes the *sacramentum Christi* and that is empowered by Christ to enact and embody his saving work. As the constitution also pointed out (CSL 28), within that assembly there are a variety of ministers and ministries which, in the ideal at least, ought not be conflated into one.

What the postconciliar movement toward a true distribution of liturgical ministries has urged upon us, not only for the Eucharist but for all sacramental rituals, is the need to specify what ministry is proper to the presiding priest and what ministries may, and indeed ought to, belong to others. Since this can be done more easily in regard to the Eucharist, a brief reflection on that may serve as paradigm for the sacrament of reconciliation.

The Roman Sacramentary makes it very clear that the specific ministry of the presider is a ministry of prayer. The presider leads the prayer of the assembly, and, most especially in the case of the Eucharist, prays the Eucharistic prayer of consecration. It is proper for others to proclaim the Word, to present the prayers and the gifts of the assembly, and even to prepare the table prior to the Eucharistic prayer. It is likewise proper for others to distribute the food of the Eucharist and to extend the Eucharistic hospitality beyond the assembly to those who are sick or otherwise unable to be present. The Eucharistic prayer, the prayer of consecration, is, however, reserved for the ministry of the presider. It is a prayer to which the assembly necessarily gives its consent, *Amen*, but it is not a prayer which all, or anyone, can or should proclaim.

The reason for this is tied in with the Trinitarian nature of Christian prayer and the specific ministry of praying *in persona Christi* that belongs to the presider. It is also a function of the requirement that liturgy signify clearly the truth of Christian faith. Christian prayer is always *with Christ to the Father in the Spirit*. By baptism all believers are united with Christ and as such are able to bring forth whatever originates from Christ, whether that which partakes of his offering, for example, intercession, or that which partakes of his love for his friends, for example, peace. It is in that sense that Thomas Aquinas reminded the Church long ago that the reason anyone can baptize is that it is Christ who baptizes, that is, Christ who unites men and women to himself.

The one movement of the mystery of Christ, however, that does not originate from Christ is the sending of the Spirit. Christ implores the Spirit and must await God's gracious gift. Christ does indeed send the Spirit but only *as received*. The Church, likewise, can only implore the Spirit in invocation, and its posture in prayer before the Spirit can only be that of a humble and grateful beggar. Our prayer demands that something "be done upon us," and it is important for our prayer that someone, *in persona Christi implorantis*, invoke the Spirit upon us.

It is the epicletic nature of the Eucharistic prayer that demands the ministry of someone established in our midst to pray *in persona Christi*. The same is true of Christian initiation. It is the epicletic nature of both the post-baptismal anointing and the sacrament of confirmation that requires an ordained bishop or presbyter (or in the case of the post-baptismal anointing, a deacon) to complete the baptismal action. It is likewise the epicletic nature of the proclamation of absolution and reconciliation that requires the ministry of one *in persona Christi*, that is, the ordained president of the assembly, for its proclamation, even if, as in the case of this suggested ritual alternative, the "gifts" are prepared and the "table" set by others.

It is not a farfetched analogy to consider in the sacrament of reconciliation that the naming of one's sins and the presentation of oneself in honesty and integrity before the Father, bring forth our baptismal truth and partake of the "preparation of the gifts." Nor is it a stretch of the imagination to see in the compassion and forgiveness embodied by the lay ministers an extension of the Eucharistic hospitality, namely, Christ's love and affection for his friends. What is missing if the liturgy is to express the full mystery of Christ (CSL 2) is the sign of epiclesis, that action of Christ imploring God's transforming Spirit to transmute sin into non-sin. For the ritual to be symbolically honest, someone must portray the *persona Christi implorantis* for us all. Such is the prime liturgical ministry of those we ordain.

The relation between the two parts of this ritual of reconciliation becomes clear if we view confession, absolution, and reconciliation against the grid of offertory, consecration, and Communion. The experience that gives rise to Part I of the ritual is truly part of the sacrament in that it exhibits and embodies both the offertory (the naming and presenting of one's sins and oneself as a sinner) and communion (the loving compassion and embrace of those made one in Christ). The second part brings forward both and completes them with the consecration (the prayer and declaration of absolution), which brings about the transformation of sin and the fullness of reconciliation.

In the preconciliar practice of private confession, the presider was asked to fulfill all the liturgical ministries required for full reconciliation, much the same as in the post-Tridentine Mass. That was a fact of the particular ritual form that was employed. An unfortunate side effect of this, however, as was indeed true of the Eucharist as well, was to forget the variety of ministers and ministries and assume that all belonged exclusively and necessarily to the ordained priest. It is crucial, as we open doors to any alternative future for worship, that we discover again that this is not so.

An additional yield of this particular alternative is the bringing together, in a way that respects the dynamics of each, and yet intimately relates them to each other, both the communal and the private dimensions of reconciliation. The reality of the Church is brought into the private arena by the one who ministers, and this same reality is returned to the community from which it always begins. In the common arena sufficient attention and respect is given to what has already happened and to the deeper truth that "what happened" in private needs completion in the prayer of the whole community. It is not just the private exchange between two people alone. Finally to respect the intensely personal nature of sin and forgiveness, the personal "I absolve you" is spoken to each individually, even though the form for general absolution is used in common.

ALTERNATIVE 3:
LITURGY FOR A CHRISTIAN DAY OF ATONEMENT

Peter E. Fink, S.J.

Introduction

In at least two of the essays contained in this volume, namely, the essay on history and that on group reconciliation, a rather significant observation has been made with regard to the sacrament of reconciliation. Throughout its history the dominant focus of this act of the Church has been upon personal sin and personal forgiveness. This remains true of the current official rituals in *The Rite of Penance*, and it is likewise true of the first two ritual alternatives presented above. There has, of course, been some inclusion of interpersonal sin and of the communal nature of reconciliation and forgiveness, but even this has been explored and addressed as a function of personal sin.

Yet the sacrament of reconciliation is about more than personal sin. Christian faith proclaims that the death and resurrection of Jesus Christ has rendered all sin, not simply personal sin, to be finally without power, and the sacrament, which is enacted in anamnesis of his death and resurrection, has as its aim the defeat and undoing of all sin, and not simply personal sin. In enacting this sacrament of reconciliation and forgiveness, the Church and Christ in the Church seek to issue a direct assault on the reality of sin in all of its manifestations.

The essay on reconciliation of groups by Denis Woods speaks of a different manifestation of sin, one which is larger and more elusive than the sins of any one person, yet quite definitely a source of division and destruction. What he is naming there is a reality which has in the contemporary world increasingly entered the consciousness of Christians and of many beyond the boundaries of Christianity. The name *social sin* has been generated to identify institutional and structural forces which produce oppression, assault the quality of human life, induce neglect of fundamental human dignity, cause alienation among groups, and, what may be their worst manifestation, stir war among peoples. It is a reality that is larger than the sum of the personal sins of the people involved. In fact, as Woods himself has pointed out, it is not infrequently contributed to by well-meaning people acting in good faith to achieve what appears to them to be a good. Yet nonetheless division and destruction result.

This kind of sin, too, cries out for the victory of Jesus Christ. It is difficult, for example, to observe starving children in Ethiopia, or to remember the Holocaust of World War II, or to note the destructiveness being heaped on people in Central America, the Middle East, and Northern Ireland and not hear the plaintive tones of Jesus' lament: "O Jerusalem, Jerusalem, the city that murders the prophets and stones the messengers sent to her! How often have I longed to gather your children, as a hen gathers her brood under her wings; but you would not let me" (Matt 23:37). It is equally difficult to see large groups of people discriminated against, nations gearing themselves up for nuclear war, and even Churches and religious peoples taking strong, sometimes violent, stances against each other on the basis of alleged religious motivation and not to hear the judgment of the God of Exodus: "I have seen the miserable state of my people in Egypt. I have heard their appeal to be free of their slave-drivers. Yes, I am well aware of their sufferings. I mean to deliver them" (3:7-8). From the cross Jesus cried out: "Father, forgive them; they do not know what they are doing" (Luke 23:34). It seems perhaps that we still do not know.

One of the clear manifestations of social sin is the division among groups that Woods has spoken about. This will be the subject of the fourth ritual alternative offered in this volume. Yet there is another aspect of social sin which does not invite any direct attempt at resolution or reconciliation but which nonetheless still challenges Christian believers to say something, and to do something, in face of it. It is that manifestation of sin which we are helpless to do anything about.

Both Woods and Roy have noted the effect on human consciousness of the culture in which people live, the culture people continue to feed and nourish by their lives and the values they choose to embrace. A real challenge to Christian people in any given culture is to hold onto and proclaim the values and truth of the Gospel as a counter-cultural critique and a force that itself may influence and shape the culture in turn. Even if there is nothing specific and concrete that immediately issues forth from rehearsing these Gospel values, it is vitally necessary that we Christians continue to do so. And this, for no other reason than to be a counter voice that may in some way or other and at some time or other stay the tide of destructiveness that may otherwise go unchallenged. We need to take this stance for ourselves as well.

The ritual alternative presented here is an attempt to shape a proper Christian stance toward and response to evil over which we have no control whatsoever. The stance itself is the thing. It can be seen as an assault on this reality of sin, at least insofar as it refuses to acquiesce in it, to ignore it, or to simply imagine it away. It is not a pragmatic ritual. It aims at no immediate result. It is a ritual for those times when there is literally nothing else we can do.

I think of an analogy between this kind of ritual on the social plane and the ritual of exorcism on the personal plane. Exorcism can seem like so much voodoo magic if we imagine that by it we are doing something pragmatic, concrete, or specific. The truth is that the ritual of exorcism is called upon, *and only called upon*, when there is literally nothing else we can do. When the resources of medicine are exhausted, when the resources of science are exhausted, when we have tried every conceivable path available to human knowledge, we can only take a stance in ignorance, and fear, and awe, in the face of evil that is beyond our control and understanding. The ritual of exorcism is such a stance. It is a surrender in hope when all else fails, all else but hope alone. It reminds us that such a surrender is not defeat but the exercise of a deeper wisdom and a deeper truth that we human beings dare not forget. The forces of evil in all their manifestations have been conquered in the death and resurrection of Christ. This is the bold proclamation of our faith, even when we do not understand the terms of this conquest or see its results in ways we recognize.

The ritual presented here is a form of exorcism on a global, rather than a personal, plane. Its intention is for social manifestations of evil what exorcism intends for personal manifestations of evil: positive hope when all else fails.

Both for our psychological growth and for our spiritual growth, we need to take such a stance in the face of our own impotence. Only the child thinks it can get everything it wants and do everything it wants to do. Only the unhealthy, in Lynch's terms, imagine that all things can be hoped for. Healthy adults know of times when they can only stand in silence before a mystery too large. They know that silence and silent hope are all they can bring to such times. Death is such a mystery; the destruction of love is such a mystery. The helpless experience of things and people "falling through the cracks" is such a mystery, as is war, the evils of oppression, the image of a starving child somehow isolated from all attempts to help. If Paul Roy gives us the challenge to grow up individually, it must also be a challenge to grow up collectively. Such growth involves an adult stance in the face of our own impotence.

The ritual alternative presented here is one attempt to address the seemingly overwhelming reality of social sin. It recognizes that social sin, even as personal and interpersonal sin, cries out for the victory of Jesus Christ. It recognizes that social sin cries out for a word of "Good News" that brings forgiveness, reconciliation, and sin's undoing. It further recognizes that social sin needs to enter into the arena of the Church's mission and ministry and its sacramental action, no less than does sin that is more personal.

Yet it is a challenge to know what dynamics should attend this address to social sin. It seems that the process of undoing personal sin is a far more manageable affair. The call to conversion in the case of personal sin has only one freedom to negotiate, and the task of undoing personal sin is limited to a very small sphere. Social sin involves not only a large number of freedoms, but often enough, and what makes it even more unmanageable, forces that are out of the control of any one person. Whereas in the case of personal sin, one can reasonably hope that something might be done about it, in the case of social sin such hope is doomed to frustration, at least if one is looking for some effect that is immediate and significant.

The inability to do anything, or at least very much, in the face of social sin changes the approach which the Church must adopt if it should seek to address social sin sacramentally with the Gospel of Christ. Judgment it may certainly bring, and a call to conversion that holds forth the values of Christ to the institution, structure, nation, or Church. But the very overwhelming nature of the task puts the Church in the position of powerlessness rather than power, of humble begging rather than confident control. These points must characterize any ritual action of the sacrament of reconciliation and forgiveness that would address social sin.

Thus the ritual alternative presented here is one of humble hope and entrustment to God. While it remains true even in the case of personal sin that God alone can bring about its undoing, the sacramentality of the Church allows it to be somewhat confident towards the healing of personal sin. In the face of social sin, however, the Church itself must come face-to-face with the deepest truth about the undoing of sin. All it may be able to bring forth is a faith and a hope and a prayer that "gives over" the reality of sin to the power of God. In the face of social sin, the Church's prayer must be eschatological prayer at its best, prayer which will urge us to do what we can, where we can, but which still allows us something hopeful to say and to do when it seems we can do nothing at all.

What is offered here, as a way to address directly the growing consciousness of social sin, is a suggestion to establish a Christian Day of Atonement on the last Saturday of the liturgical year, that is, on the Saturday before the celebration of Christ the King. The nature of this particular feast as the proclamation of Christ's Lordship over all history, all structures, all institutions, indeed all creation itself, identifies it as the most appropriate time to consider such an event of prayer and liturgical action. What is envisioned is a day of fast and repentance on which the Christian community will offer its prayer for God's forgiveness and healing of sins that are elusive to personal grasp. Included in this are the sins of the community itself, the sins of the Church, and the sins of the world.

The idea is inspired by the Jewish Day of Atonement. It acknowledges that the reality of sin is something larger than sins of individuals and requires a healing beyond that of individual reconciliation. Unlike the Jewish Day of Atonement, however, it is not comprised of several sacrificial offerings. For Christians there is only the one saving sacrifice of Jesus Christ, the victory of which needs to be tapped for the good of all. The principal act of the Church on a Christian Day of Atonement will be to place the sins of the community, the Church, and the world within the sacrificial offering of Jesus Christ. Only when they are so placed can they hope to be healed and transformed by the loving action of God. In prayer the Church remembers the God who in Christ reconciled the world to himself, entrusts the world to this God, and seeks itself to be transformed to the ministry of reconciliation.

The ritual offered here is given in three parts. There is first a solemn opening of the Day of Atonement for Friday evening to take place in the assembly of the local parish church. The second part offers a collection of table prayers to be used at home on both Friday and Saturday evenings. The third, briefest of all, is an introductory rite to open the liturgy of Christ the King. This festive liturgy brings the Day of Atonement to a conclusion.

RITE OF RECONCILIATION

Part I: Solemn Opening of the Day of Atonement

The ritual takes place in church. The altar is bare except for a cross and a thurible with coals burning.

GATHERING

The assembly gathers on Friday evening. The presider and ministers take their places in silence.

OPENING CHANT

At the appointed time the cantor or choir chants the *Kyrie eleison* slowly and prayerfully, using a tone appropriate to the occasion.

READING: Matt 23:37-39

PSALM: All *kneel* and sing Ps 130.

R̸. I place all my trust in you, my God;
all my hope is in your mercy.

OPENING PRAYER

The presider stands for the prayer; all others remain kneeling.

Presider: My brothers and sisters in Christ,
let us pray:

God of mercy and compassion,
look graciously upon the world which you have
made,
and on the people who are won for you
by the blood of your Son, Jesus Christ.

Our sins are many; make them white as snow.

Bathe us once more in the blood of the Lamb,
that, by your power,
all the wounds we inflict on each other
may be healed,
and all the scars we mark upon the earth
may be taken away.

We ask this through Jesus Christ, our Lord,
who lives and rules with you and the Holy
    Spirit,
one God, forever and ever.

All: Amen.

All are seated.

Liturgy of the Word

READING: Hos 6:1-6

RESPONSORIAL PSALM: Ps 95

℟. If today you hear his voice, harden not your
hearts.

READING: 2 Cor 5:16-21

GOSPEL ACCLAMATION

Alleluia . . .
Let us glory in the cross of our Lord Jesus
    Christ.
He saves us and sets us free;
through him we find salvation, life, and
    resurrection.
Alleluia . . . .

GOSPEL: John 13:1-10

HOMILY

Solemn Rite of Atonement

Several basins of water to be used in the ceremony of cleansing are
brought before the presider for blessing as the atonement prayer begins. During the rite of washing, several ministers will be needed
with towels to assist the people.

Presider: My sisters and brothers,
in solemn prayer we open this Day of
Atonement.
Our eyes are turned to the Crucified One
whose death has broken the bonds of sin and
death.

Before the power of our own sin
and the sin of others
we stand helpless.
We have no place to turn but to him
who is mercy itself.

This night we pray to the Lord of all
to blot out and pardon our own sin,
and all the sins upon the earth.
We place ourselves at the mercy of our God
who alone can reconcile the world to the Godhead.

Let us ask God's blessing on this water
that it may bring to us,
to our Church and to our world,
the cleansing grace of our Lord Jesus Christ.

Pause for silent prayer.

Gracious and loving God,
on this night of holy atonement,
we ask you to breathe your mercy on this water
that it be for us
the forgiveness of our sin,
the healing of all division,
and the dawn of your life within us.

Send your Spirit upon us
and upon the water of this font.
May all of us who are washed with your water
of life
find in your mercy pardon and peace.

We ask this through Christ, our Lord.

All: Amen.

PRAYER FOR THE LOCAL COMMUNITY

Presider: Let us pray now, my brothers and sisters,
that our own sins may be taken away.

Let us entrust our life together
as a community of believers in Christ
to the tender mercy of our God.

All kneel. A member of the community, or one of the ministers, comes to the altar and places some incense on the coals in the thurible. The presider begins the *Confiteor* and all join in.

Presider: Let us acknowledge our sins before God and
each other:

All: I confess to almighty God . . . .

Presider: May Almighty God have mercy on us,
forgive us our sins,
and bring us to life everlasting.

All: Amen.

Presider: Please come forward, and with hearts contrite,
bathe your hands in the forgiveness of our God.

All in the assembly come forward, wash their hands in the water that has been blessed, and return to their places. During this ritual washing, an appropriate song or psalm, such as Ps 51, may be sung.

When all have returned to their places, they kneel.

Presider: (standing with hands extended over the assembly)

Merciful God,
we place our sins and all their harmful effects
into the offering of your Son, Jesus Christ.
We ask you to heal and transform them
with the same power
with which you raised Jesus from the dead.

As once you formed us to be your people,
we ask you now
to heal the wounds that divide us
and pardon all our sins.

Bind us more deeply in faith, hope, and love,
that we may be signs of your healing grace
to all upon the earth.

We ask this through Christ, our Lord.

All: Amen.

All are seated.

PRAYER FOR THE CHURCH

Presider: And now, my sisters and brothers,
let us ask the mercy and forgiveness of God
upon our Church.

We are broken and divided,
though the Lord asks us to be one.
We are touched by spots of blindness,
though the Lord has opened our eyes.
We are not without our own moments of
    darkness
though the Lord has called us light for the
    world.

Mixed with the wheat of God's gracious work
    among us
remain the weeds of our own sin.
For our Church, weak and divided,
let us ask the atonement of Christ.

In silence, a member of the assembly goes forward to place, for a
second time, some incense in the thurible.
All stand.

Leader: For the Church throughout the world,
let us pray to the Lord:

R̸. Lord, have mercy.

That divisions may cease among us,
let us pray to the Lord: R̸.

That we may learn the unity for which Christ
    prayed,
let us pray to the Lord: R̸.

That our hearts may be opened
to the fullness of Christ's word,
let us pray to the Lord: R̸.

That the grip of our pride may be loosened
by the power of the humble Christ,
let us pray to the Lord: R̸.

That our selfishness be transformed
into generous love and service,
let us pray to the Lord: R̸.

That we never use power to abuse or oppress,
let us pray to the Lord: R̨.

That we may be purified of our sins:
those we see, and those to which we are blind,
let us pray to the Lord: R̨.

Presider: O tender and compassionate God,
we ask that you be merciful
to your Church throughout the world.
Brighten our darkness,
and make us your radiant bride.
Heal our divisions,
and weave us into your seamless robe.
Cast from us all signs of unwelcome,
and make us your holy temple
where you, our God, will be pleased to dwell.

We ask this through Christ, our Lord.

All: Amen.

All are seated. As a symbol of the Church being cleansed, the four
faces of the altar are now washed by members of the assembly.
Meanwhile, the assembly or choir sings the *Trisagion* which may
be chanted in the vernacular alone or in addition to Greek and Latin
as well.

All: Hagios o Theos, hagios ischyros, hagios
athanatos eleison imas.

Sanctus Deus, sanctus fortis, sanctus immortalis,
miserere nobis.

Holy God, holy mighty One, holy immortal
One, have mercy on us.

The chant continues until the washing of the altar is completed.

PRAYER FOR THE WORLD

Presider: My brothers and sisters,
we are one with the people of the earth.
In this final prayer of atonement,
we raise our voices for God's gracious mercy
upon north and south, and east and west,
upon all nations, all peoples,
and all creation itself.

For a third time, a member of the assembly approaches the altar and places incense on the coals.

All stand.

All: God of all the nations,
God of the heavens and the earth,
our voice is the voice of all creation
as it yearns for deliverance.

Loosen the bonds that entrap us.
Release us from every power of evil
that sets nation against nation,
sister against brother, parent against child.

We scatter your healing waters
to the four corners of the earth
and raise our voice in humble prayer.

Hear the deep sighs and groans
from within your creation itself,
and speedily bring to all people
the redemption your Son has gained for us.

We ask this through Christ, our Lord.

Amen.

The presider sprinkles water to the north, south, east, and west, proclaiming in a loud voice:

Presider: Christ yesterday and today,
the beginning and the end,
Alpha and Omega.
All time belongs to him
and all the ages.
To him be glory and power
through every age, forever.

At the conclusion of the sprinkling and proclamation, the assembly joins in a suitable song of praise and dedication.

Concluding Rite

Presider: Let us now join together in the prayer
which Jesus taught us:

All: Our Father . . . . But deliver us from evil.
For the kingdom . . . forever and ever. Amen.

Presider:	Our Day of Atonement has begun. Let us go forth to keep the fast and to pray with united voice for the healing mercy of our God.
	And may God's blessing go with you, + Father, Son, and Holy Spirit.
All:	Amen.

Since this service opens out on the day of fasting, no concluding song is necessary. However, if a song is sung, it should be in a tone proper to the beginning of a day of fast and prayer.

Part II: Table Prayers for the Home

The following prayers are adapted from the previous service in order to show the continuity between the liturgical service and prayer in the home during this solemn Day of Atonement. The table prayers constitute a short prayer service to be offered at the beginning of the evening meal on both Friday and Saturday nights. In place of the incense and water used in the church service, three candles are set on the table. They will be lighted in turn as each of the petitions is prayed.

CALL TO PRAYER

Leader:	On this night of atonement we seek the mercy of our God.
	We stand helpless before the power of our own sin and the sin of others.
	On this night we pray to the Lord of all to pardon our sins and the sins of all the world.

PRAYER FOR THE LOCAL COMMUNITY

Let us pray, first of all,
for our family gathered here,
([OR:] for our table gathering)
that God will heal us
from the harm we bring to each other.

The first candle is lighted in silence.

> Merciful God,
> we place our sins as a family
> ([OR:] we place our sins as friends and
>   neighbors)
> into the offering of your Son, Jesus Christ.
> We ask you to heal the wounds we inflict on
>   each other,
> and give us your pardon and your peace.
>
> In your mercy forgive us all our sins:

All: R7. Have mercy on us, O Lord!

> Teach us your ways of love and life: R7.

PRAYER FOR THE CHURCH

Leader: Let us pray too for the Church throughout the
>   world,
> that all divisions may cease,
> and that the salvation won by Jesus Christ
> may come to all people.

The second candle is lighted in silence.

> O tender and compassionate God,
> be merciful to us, your Church.
> Heal our divisions.
> Brighten our darkness.
> Make us a holy temple
> where you, our God, will be pleased to dwell.
>
> In your mercy forgive us all our sins:

All: R7. Have mercy on us, O Lord!

> Teach us your ways of love and life: R7.

PRAYER FOR THE WORLD

Leader: Let us now ask God's mercy and love
> for all peoples upon the earth.

The third candle is lighted in silence.

> God of all the nations;
> God of heaven and of earth!
> Hear the voice of your creation
> as it yearns for deliverance.

Release us from every force
that sets nation against nation,
sister against brother, parent against child;
and give to all peoples of the earth
your own lasting peace.

In your mercy forgive us all our sins:

All: ℟. Have mercy on us, O Lord!

Teach us your ways of love and life: ℟.

BLESSING BEFORE THE MEAL

Bless us, Lord, and this food we share,
and grant your mercy to us all
through Christ, our Lord.

All: Amen.

The meal is now shared.

THANKSGIVING AFTER THE MEAL

All: Christ yesterday and today,
the beginning and the end,
Alpha and Omega.
All time belongs to him
and all the ages.
To him be glory and power
through every age forever.
Amen.

Part III: Introductory Rite for Sunday's Liturgy

After the usual greeting of the assembly:

Presider: My sisters and brothers,
we bring our day of atonement to completion
at the throne of Christ
who is Lord and king of all.

We open our prayer in praise of him
who is God's mercy upon the earth.

Lord Jesus, Mercy of the Father,
in you all sins are forgiven.
Lord, have mercy.

All: Lord, have mercy.

Presider:	Christ Jesus, gracious gift of pardon, you have been sent to gather all the nations, Christ, have mercy.
All:	Christ, have mercy.
Presider:	Lord Jesus, Word of God's compassion, come, heal us now, that we may praise you always. Lord, have mercy.
All:	Lord, have mercy.
Presider:	May almighty God have mercy on us, forgive us our sins, and lead us to life everlasting.
All:	Amen.

The Liturgy of the Eucharist continues as usual.

Commentary: Content

The ritual suggested here is, as noted in the introduction, inspired by the Jewish Day of Atonement. That day of solemn fast came into being from the need to purge the Temple and the people from their sins and from a firm recognition that God alone had the power to do this. It is not a pragmatic feast, one which lines up an expected outcome and expects that outcome to come about. It is worship at its most pure, a surrender of all human impotence to the omnipotence of the Creator.

Whereas the Jewish ritual called for the sprinkling of blood to effect the purification, this ritual calls on the water of Christian baptism. Incense is burned as our prayer of offering and invocation, while water, which purified us all at birth and incorporated us into the mystery of Christ's sacrifice, seeks to incorporate the assembly, the Church, and indeed all creation into the mystery of Christ's saving grace. The actions speak our deepest yearnings and at the same time God's own deepest yearnings for us.

As a solemn ritual, the first part is envisioned to take place in a parish assembly. At the same time, as an opening on to a day of fast, the ritual is but a piece of a larger task for that parish assembly. It is not meant to "accomplish" anything except, as is true of all good sacramental ritual, *significando*, that is, by signifying. Its true power, and the power of the day of fast itself, lies in its ability to change our consciousness and the hardness of our hearts.

It will be successful if it invites us, allows us, and shapes us to take even the darkest evil in the world and offer it in worship to our God. Such an act may or may not affect the evil reality; it will certainly affect its power. Evil that can be embraced in worship of God is finally not humanly destructive, but rather positively contributes to our human wholeness before God. Such, it should be said, is the deepest revelation of a crucified Christ.

As a ritual of surrender, it is a perfect "vigil" for the Feast of Christ the King. Together with that festive celebration, it brings the year to its proper conclusion, combining into a single hymn of praise both earnest prayer for purification and even more earnest acknowledgement that Christ is for all and all is for Christ.

Since the suggestion here is in harmony with the Jewish feast that also comes at the "end of the year," the hope is to plug into that human mood of gratitude and regret that comes with yearly endings. The problem, of course, is that neither the time for Yom Kippur nor the time for Christ the King is a genuine year's end. Could this suggestion be more successful on December 31, or perhaps the end of the summer? If the idea itself has any merit, the proper time to enact it may well be other than that suggested here.

The flow of the ritual is self-evident in the text. The readings are all chosen to proclaim God's deepest desires for creation and to invite us into those deepest desires. The personal hand washing, which I have used in a parish retreat on reconciliation, is effective, far more so than the customary sprinkling of water over the assembly. The washing of the altar to represent the washing of the Church has equally shown itself to have power. It echoes the Temple purification, and reminds us that the Church too needs to be purified. Finally, the third sprinkling, to the four corners of the globe, is a mere suggestion, yet not without its own suggestive power. It can serve at least until, with use, a better ritual expression might be devised.

The table prayers for use at home are important, both to give structure to the day of fast at hand and to bring the Church's ritual prayer into the home. Christian prayer is weak on home celebrations, and the linking of public prayer with home prayer may serve as a model to create more prayer forms for home use.

Finally, the acclamations to be included in the Introductory Rites for the feast of Christ the King properly close the day of fast, and allow the Eucharistic celebration of the feast to be seen as its proper completion.

The first question that must be asked of a ritual suggestion such as the one proposed here is an honest, "Will it fly?" Is it something that will touch a sufficient chord in the hearts of the people for whom it is proposed as to allow it to speak to their yearnings and their faith? Or is it little more than a suggestion from on high, interesting to scholar and ritual composer, but with little or no point of intersection with the experience of ordinary people? The latter alternative is certainly a danger which must be honestly acknowledged. An answer to the first question is "possibly," at least in some form or other, depending on a certain number of conditions.

One condition would be that people are sufficiently sensitive to the reality of social sin as a destructive reality in and to the world that they find in their own lives some need to address that sin with the power of Christ. People whose only sense of sin is personal, or possibly interpersonal in a very narrow range, and who are quite comfortable in dismissing the larger issues of structural oppression, social degradation, and war as "the way things are" will find the suggestion offered here irrelevant at best and at worst positively annoying. A second condition would be for people to understand that the undoing of sin is not in our power at all, and that even where we can do something about it, that something arises from God and not from ourselves. People of a pragmatic and political bent who want things to change *now*, or else nothing worthwhile is actually happening, will find the ritual too passive for their tastes. It can seem like a slip back to the days when we casually left all to God.

This ritual of Christian atonement will speak positively where a deep sense of the evil of social sin is present, where there is a deep realization that we are helpless to do much in the face of social sin, and where the faith-filled and hope-filled act of entrustment to God is seen to be a positive act at the point of powerlessness and not an irresponsible excuse for not doing anything to change things. It is not without precedent in the history of the Christian people to suggest fasting and prayer in the face of evils too large.

A second question must also be asked: "Should it fly?" Is there any reason to consider this suggestion seriously even for those who want to dismiss it as "Ivory Tower," needless, or irrelevant? I find myself a bit bolder in answering this one, and I give a very definite yes. Where the consciousness of social sin is strong, a ritual of this kind can serve to keep before people *both* the challenge to do whatever they can to undo it *and* the power of Christ's own surrender to social evil where they can do nothing else. Hope in the face of evil may well be evil's radical undoing. On the other hand, where the consciousness of social sin is not strong and where people are comfortable simply to acquiesce in it, a ritual of this kind can serve a prophetic function, a call to consciousness and an assault on the very acquiescence which is evil's own victory. Whether in the form of a Day of Christian Atonement or in some other ritual form, Christians need to address the evils of social sin and seek to render them if not non-existent, at least impotent.

ALTERNATIVE 4:
LITURGY FOR THE RECONCILIATION OF GROUPS

Peter E. Fink, S.J., and Denis J. Woods

Introduction

Our efforts at imagining alternative futures for the sacrament of reconciliation would not be complete without some attempt to address the challenge posed earlier in this volume in the essay on the reconciliation of groups. The challenge may be simply put: Is it possible to imagine any ritual forms that will serve this complex and fragile process as the process unfolds, and is it possible to construct a ritual to seal and celebrate its success, when indeed success is achieved?

It is a challenge that must be met in some way or other if the premise of this work is to hold true, namely, that in the victory of Christ's resurrection, all sources of division and alienation have been overcome, and a power to bring about reconciliation wherever alienation and division occur has been definitively unleashed upon the world. Yet it is a challenge that must be met with extreme care and bold honesty: care, because the process itself is so difficult and delicate; and honesty, because there is so much in the process that ritual cannot do and should not pretend to be able to do.

Even in beginning to move to meet the challenge, the full complexity and delicacy of the process by which groups may be helped toward reconciliation must be borne in mind. Each of the three levels of divisions among groups mentioned earlier, namely, distributive divisions, ideological divisions, and structural divisions, has its own peculiar set of obstacles to be overcome and its own level of difficulty with regard to the reconciliation process. The prospect of achieving reconciliation grows less as these obstacles become more resistant to any efforts to overcome them and as the nature of the division itself conceals the truth of its own divisiveness. As already mentioned, more hope may be given to the possibility of reconciliation in the case of distributive divisions than in the case of ideological or structural divisions. But however high the level of difficulty and however low the level of hope, the process must be pursued in all cases by a Church that claims to have been given by Christ the mission and mandate to reconcile.

Before the question of ritual can be addressed, the nature of the ministry of reconciliation in the cases of group division and alienation needs to be explored. The ritual question will be properly located and resolved only as a function of that ministry. Just as the process itself involves far more than ritual, assuming that ritual may have any place in the process at all, so too the ministry to the process involves far more than questions of ritual. It involves presence, a commitment of time and energy and affection, enormous patience, attentiveness to any signs of breakthrough that may be captured and capitalized upon, and a vision, a hope, and a dream. The ministry to the reconciliation process will itself determine if, and how, ritual of any kind might enter the process successfully.

One crucial element of the ministry involved in the reconciliation of groups is that it is a ministry of *presence*, of "being *with*." This presence as "one who is with" is essential. One cannot hope to serve the reconciliation process if one's own ministry becomes itself an instrument of division. Since it is ministry, there is a sense in which it is also a "being for," but this cannot have any nuances of superiority or condescension about it. The minister can only be "for" by being "with," that is, by suspending his or her own agenda always in favor of the agenda which the groups themselves bring to the surface. Any hopes, dreams, or wisdom which the minister may bring to the process must be allowed to surface among the groups themselves *as their own*.

In addition this ministry may at times find it necessary to take the shape of "being over-against" in a kind of prophetic stance. But this too must always be in the *prior* context of "being with." By itself, "being over-against" is divisive and therefore potentially a hindrance to reconciliation. However it may at times be helpful to stand over-against in a prophetic mode, "being with" must always remain primary. Only by "being with" can the minister preserve and serve the freedom, the integrity, and the dignity of the people who are served, something which is as necessary for group reconciliation as it is for individual reconciliation.

A second element in the ministry to the reconciliation of groups involves finding something which the divided groups have in common. Without this there will be nothing to ground or urge the reconciliation. This "something" can wear a variety of faces.

In the case of distributive divisions, for example, it could be simply the realization that both groups will be out of a job unless some reconciliation is achieved. Both sides will therefore have some stake in achieving reconciliation. In the case of ideological divisions, such as occur over the abortion issue, it may be the realization that by holding to a standoff on the ideological plane, neither side is exerting any real influence on the political arena, where the issue is in fact being resolved in law. Locked in a world where they are only shouting at each other, they have removed themselves from the world where real difference is being made. In a winner-take-all battle the so-called victory of the winner needs to be exposed as only an illusory victory.

Most difficult of all is the level of structural division. Here the common ground may well be simply the realization that the structural flaw which is at the root of the division is in fact harming both sides and not simply one. To those who are on the "up" side of structural division, this will not be immediately apparent.

The key in all cases is to locate something they have in common, be it a common history, a common value, a common need, a common hope, or even a common loss they are both experiencing in the division. It is, in Macmurray's terms, the positive that will relativize and lure beyond the various negatives that divide. It must be something that is seen to be of greater value to both and therefore worth pursuing beyond the lesser values that when held onto reinforce division and alienation. This discovery of common ground must be done from "within."

The appearance of this "something" which they have in common cannot be scheduled or forced, and this suggests yet a third element in the ministry to the reconciliation of groups. Paul's term *kairos* is important here. Careful attention on the part of the minister to "seize the moment" when the groups can themselves be helped to "seize the moment" is perhaps the single most important ministry that can be brought to the process. Bad timing could result in "the moment lost." Or it could result in the appearance, at least, of an agenda being foisted upon the groups rather than *seized upon by them.*

A final element in the ministry of group reconciliation which we would mention is linked to the *kairos.* Here it is not so much a case of seizing the moment for the possibility of some measure of reconciliation. Rather it is a case of latching onto and celebrating whatever measure of success, however small, is in fact achieved. This would certainly include making much of the full reconciliation if indeed such should occur. But it also includes, and with the same degree of importance and value, any positive steps that bring the full reconciliation closer to being realized.

This brief listing of some essential characteristics of the ministry of group reconciliation helps to locate the possible place or places where ritual action might contribute positively to the process. It should be clear that the inclusion of ritual acts within the process of reconciliation of groups and the construction of ritual acts to serve that process are complex and delicate issues, as is the process itself. It should also be clear that any such ritual can only be included as part of the ministry to the people involved.

Ritual cannot have a life independent of the process, or else it will be simply irrelevant to the process and its success. It cannot be imposed as an agenda from without or in any way attempt to manipulate the process or its outcome. Ritual is service, not manipulation. And as service ritual too must arise from "within" the process, not from without. This will make any ritual suggested here only an example or model to guide the shaping of an actual ritual which the reconciliation process itself would have to generate from within.

As service to the process of reconciliation, ritual must be a function of *kairos.* It is almost impossible to program in the abstract the precise function or functions ritual may serve. Here, too, suggestions must be at best suggestive.

It is possible that ritual may serve in a prophetic role even before the process begins, as an invitation and a challenge to change divisive ways. But this would probably be a true option only where the groups involved already share a common history which allows them together to be vulnerable to the invitation and challenge. In such a case, for example, a division within a local parish or a division among Christian Churches, it is the common history, which they already share, that grounds the possibility of prophecy. In such instances the prophecy itself would then arise from "within." Where there is no such common reality which is already shared, such a prophetic act would come, as it were, from without, "over-against," and as such its value toward reconciliation would most likely be minimal if indeed it had any value at all.

The value of ritual in the reconciliation of groups will probably not surface unless and until some common ground is established. At that point it could then serve a most helpful role in the process, namely, to solidify and to "keep in remembrance" that common ground. It could serve to hold out what is common as the primary context in which the process will continue to unfold. It could serve to solidify commitment to what is common and in turn give this common ground increased power. A ritual celebration at this point would raise the common ground to the level of "common myth," with all the power myth has to claim allegiance, shape motivation, urge decision, and invite people towards its realization.

Thus two possible ritual moments can be envisioned: one to establish and celebrate the common ground, and thereby raise it to the level of common myth, and one, much briefer, to hold this common myth "in remembrance" as the context for the ongoing deliberations. This latter could be in the form of a prayer, a Scripture text, or a simple story at the beginning of deliberation sessions.

A second place for ritual enactment in the ongoing process would certainly be those times when some measure of advance toward reconciliation has been achieved. This need not be a different ritual form from the one which established the common myth in the first place. In fact, it would probably best be envisioned as a recommitment to the common myth and a grateful recognition that some measure of success has been achieved. A single ritual structure that would see several enactments as the ongoing process unfolds would probably serve the process best.

A final place for the enactment of ritual, of course, would be the completion of the process, when, and if, reconciliation is in fact achieved. Several characteristics of such a ritual have already been given in the earlier essay. One is that it should emphasize responsibility, rather than guilt, and include a moment where each group could claim its own responsibility in the division they both seek to heal. A second would be an acknowledgement on the part of each group of what is good and praiseworthy in the other. A third would be a ritual form that allows people to "face their former adversaries and weep together, forgive, begin to trust each other and swear for the future." Most helpful would be the visibility to each other of the other's determination for the future.

All of this leads to the ritual suggestions being offered here. There are two. One is a basic ritual structure to celebrate the common ground, when it is agreed upon and given some measure of commitment, and to capture this agreement and commitment as a significant sacramental moment in the reconciliation process. This same ritual structure can be followed throughout the process at those points where some measure of success calls for a celebration. As will be suggested in the text, an abbreviated version of this may be a useful inclusion in the deliberations to help everyone remember the common quest, its promise, and its achievement. The second is a ritual form for forgiveness and reconciliation when the process has successfully come to a close.

These rituals are offered as the sacrament of reconciliation, that is, an action of the Church under the Word of God which effectively speaks God's forgiveness in Christ and the power of Christ's resurrection to overcome all forces of alienation and division. It is ritual in the context of faith and not simply in the context of group process. It therefore employs Christian prayer, Christian proclamation, and the language and gesture of the Christian liturgical assembly. It is the purpose of this work to stretch the Christian sacramental tradition into the arena of group reconciliation and forgiveness. This particular ritual suggestion, therefore, would be useful and useable only in that arena of faith where both alienation and the process of reconciliation are placed under the power of Jesus Christ.

It must be acknowledged, however, that alienation among groups and the need for reconciliation of groups are not restricted to the Christian community but are wider and more inclusive in their scope. In its strict sense the sacrament of reconciliation cannot include those who are not numbered among the baptized. In the wider sense, however, the term does include any and all efforts on the part of the Church to achieve reconciliation among people, whatever, if any, their religious affiliation. A Christian minister may be motivated by the Gospel of Christ and yet be unable to employ the language of that Gospel in the specific reconciliation process at hand. The ministry itself is a "being with"; its ritual form must also be a "being with."

It is necessary, therefore, to imagine the ritual forms suggested here beyond their own specific Christian contours and as potentially helpful to the process even where less specific language of God, e.g., as a "Higher Power," and less specific "humanitarian" language must be employed. The Gospel of Christ unveils a view of the human which presumably may appeal to all people of goodwill, even if they do not subscribe to and are not otherwise helped by the particular religious vision which the Gospel unfolds. Rituals employed beyond the boundaries of the Christian Church may not be the sacrament in the strict sense. In the broader sense of the term, however, they certainly could be.

At any rate, both this distinction and this connection must be borne in mind. Without the distinction this ritual suggestion could easily be dismissed as human ritual for a human process but not a proper extension of the strict sacramental practice of the Church. We do not want to facilitate such a dismissal. Without the connection, on the other hand, what is offered here will be dismissed as irrelevant to most of the alienation and division that exists among groups. We do not want to facilitate that dismissal either. However specific with Christian detail this ritual suggestion may be, and however well or poorly it may succeed in the service it hopes to render, we cannot forget the scope of the reconciling mission entrusted to the Church. It is not restricted to Christians, nor even simply to religious peoples. This mission is for all and will not be complete until all division is stamped out upon the earth.

RITE OF RECONCILIATION

Part I

This ritual form, Part I, is suggested to celebrate and solidify the discovery of something which divided groups hold in common, to celebrate and solidify a commitment on the part of each to that common bond, and to inaugurate with prayer and blessing the new phase in the reconciliation process which begins when groups do in fact discover and choose to pursue what they have in common.

The ritual is outlined in stark structure. A vessel with burning coals should be prepared in a suitable place with incense available nearby. A single large candle should be placed in the midst of the assembly with two smaller candles available for representatives of the two groups. Any other questions about environment and the particular setting for the ritual, as well as any embellishments in terms of music and gesture, will need to be determined by the groups in accordance with their own particular circumstances.

OPTION A

Option A is used when the commitment to common ground is first made and celebrated.

Introductory Rites

GATHERING

Presider: My brothers and sisters in Christ!

We come together to give thanks and rejoice
in God's gift to us.

Our time together
has yielded insight and wisdom,
hope and understanding,
and a firm grasp on something which unites us
in the face of all that divides.

It is the realization that . . .
[the common ground is briefly named].

It is a beginning, and in that beginning
we place our hope.

Let us open our prayer together
by giving praise and glory to God.

All: Glory be to the Father . . . .

Presider: May the peace and blessing of our God,
who is the source of all reconciliation
be with us.

All: Amen.

OPENING PRAYER

Presider: Let us pray:

Good and merciful God,
source of all wisdom and insight,
gift of forgiveness and promise of peace,
look with kindness upon us
and on the work we have undertaken in your
name.

Though the walls that divide us remain strong,
you have given us a glimpse through those walls.

> You have given us hope that they can be
> toppled.
>
> In gratitude and hope
> we ask that you stay with us on our journey,
> till we find, with your help,
> the reconciliation you hold out to us.
>
> We ask this together
> through Christ, our Lord.

All: Amen.

Liturgy of the Word

More appropriate readings may arise from the needs and desires of the groups involved. The following are offered by way of suggestion:

READING: Eph 4:1-6 [or] 1 Cor 1:10-25

HOMILY

Rite of Commitment to Common Ground

Presider: You have come together before God
and in the midst of this assembly
to claim and to affirm a common bond
which may lead to reconciliation
beyond all that divides you.

That bond, named among you,
is now yours to claim,
yours to affirm,
yours to follow wherever it may lead.

If you are ready to make this commitment
before God and before us all
please stand,
and let someone from each group
speak the common ground
which both acknowledge and profess.

The rite continues with the *Response* on p. 157f.

OPTION B

Option B is used when the ritual is repeated in the course of the reconciliation process.

Introductory Rites

GATHERING

Presider: My brothers and sisters in Christ!

We come together to embrace and rejoice
in God's new gift to us.

Our time together continues to yield
insight and wisdom,
hope and understanding,
and an ever more firm grasp on that which
    unites us
in the face of all that still divides.

Today we rejoice in a new bond of reconciliation
that has been given to us.
[This new bond may be mentioned here.]

It is once again a time of new beginning,
and in this new sign of God's gracious help
    among us
we continue to place our hope.

Let us open our new prayer together
by giving praise and glory to God.

All: Glory be to the Father . . . .

Presider: And may the peace and blessing of our God,
who is the source of all reconciliation
continue to be with us.

All: Amen.

OPENING PRAYER

Presider: Let us pray:

Good and merciful God,
source of all wisdom and insight,
gift of forgiveness and promise of peace
look with kindness upon us
and on the work we continue in your name.

Though the walls that divide us remain strong,
again you have given us a glimpse through those
    walls.

Again you have given us hope that they can
  be toppled.

In gratitude and hope
we ask that you stay with us on our journey
till we find, with your help,
the full reconciliation which you hold out to us.

We ask this together
through Christ, our Lord.

All: Amen.

Liturgy of the Word

More appropriate readings may arise from the needs and desires of
the groups involved. The following are offered by way of suggestion:

READING: 2 Cor 5:16-20 [or] John 17:6-19

HOMILY

Rite of Recommitment to Common Ground

INVITATION

Presider: You have come together before God
and in the midst of this assembly
to claim and to affirm once again
the common bond which you share.

You come to acknowledge with heartfelt thanks
that you are closer now to reconciliation
than when you first began.

God indeed has been good in your midst,
and you have been open
to God's work among you.

May I invite someone from each group
to come forward
and name and claim this new common ground
that has been given to us to share together.

The rite continues with the *Response* below.

RESPONSE

A representative of each group comes forward and speaks in turn,
naming the common ground to which each will be committed, or
the new level of reconciliation that has been achieved.

Presider: May God who has begun this good work in our
                  midst
                  graciously bring it to completion.

All: Amen.

INSTRUCTION

It would be difficult, if not impossible, to give even a sample instruction at this point, since it needs to be done in light of the specific
dispute in question, in light of the common ground that is decided
upon and claimed, and in light of the actual level of reconciliation
that has been achieved.

The action and commitment of both sides in the dispute should be
named here in terms of their significance in God's work of reconciliation. The common ground and the reconciliation achieved should
be located squarely in Christ's work of reconciliation, and should
affirm or reaffirm the part each group will play in that work.

PRAYER

Presider: Let us pray now in silence
                  for the continued blessings of God
                  upon our common endeavors,
                      that all divisions may in God's time be healed
                  and that God may be blessed and
                      praised.

As the assembly prays silently, representatives from each group come
forward and place incense on the burning coals. The incense itself
will speak the silent prayer of all. It may be an even more expres-
sive symbol if the representative of each side gives the incense to
the representative of the other side before the incense is placed on
the coals.

Presider: (with hands extended above the representatives:)
                  Good and gracious God,
                  we have no power to love or forgive
                  unless you yourself place that power
                  within our hearts.

                  We have no power to understand, to respect,
                  and to rejoice in the differences
                  that are ours
                  unless your Spirit within us calls us
                  to a deeper and more abiding reconciliation.

> Send this Spirit upon us once again
> to lead us more firmly to that hope
> for which your own Son prayed:
> that we be one in you.
>
> We make this prayer through Christ, our Lord.

All: Amen.

Concluding Rite

Presider: And now let us pray
as our Lord Jesus Christ has taught us to pray:

All: Our Father . . . . But deliver us from evil.
For the kingdom . . . forever and ever. Amen.

Presider: With great hope and confidence
in the Lord's work among us,
let us greet each other in peace.

Note: As part of the ongoing process toward reconciliation, at the beginning of each deliberation session, some part of the above ritual may be repeated, e.g., the prayer, the instruction, or the passage from Scripture.

Part II

Part II is intended to ritualize the completion of the reconciliation process. Unlike Part I, in which the tonalities of hope and commitment were stressed, Part II stresses acknowledgement and responsibility and mutual forgiveness. Since the ritual is interpreted as the sacrament of reconciliation in the strict sense, it must also include a prayer and proclamation of God's forgiveness.

Introductory Rites

GATHERING

Presider: My brothers and sisters in Christ:

It is indeed a great work of God in our midst
which brings us together to celebrate.

A long journey has come to an end,
and we can taste the victory that is ours.

The walls that have divided you
have been brought to the ground;

the common bond which has been your guide
has shown itself to be strong.

You gather now to give thanks to God,
to ask forgiveness of each other,
and to know that as you forgive each other
so God forgives you all.

May the peace of God,
who is Father, Son, and Spirit,
be with you.

All: And also with you.

OPENING PRAYER

Presider: Let us pray:

Lord, our God,
hear the prayers of those who call on you.
Forgive the divisions they have nurtured,
and give them large hearts to forgive each other.

You have led them to this time of reconciliation.
For this we give you praise and thanks.

By the power that is at work within us
you are able to do more than anything
we can ask or imagine.
To you be honor and glory
in the Church and in Christ Jesus,
now and forever.

All: Amen.

Liturgy of the Word

READING: Isa 55:6-13

RESPONSORIAL PSALM: Ps 8

℟. O Lord, our Lord, how glorious is your
name in all the earth!

READING: Rom 6:1-11

GOSPEL ACCLAMATION: John 13:34

Alleluia . . .
A new commandment I give to you,

that you love one another as I have loved you.
Alleluia . . . .

GOSPEL: John 15:9-17

HOMILY

Rite of Reconciliation

INVITATION

Presider: My brothers and sisters in Christ:

We come to the time of forgiveness and
      reconciliation,
a time of honesty before God
and before one another.

We are sinners, each and all:
this is our common truth.
And we are forgiven by God, each and all:
this is the revelation of Jesus Christ to us.

On this day of healing grace,
when groups once divided
have found a way to be one,
I would ask
that someone come forward
to speak for each group:

to acknowledge and claim responsibility
for the divisions that have been so costly;
to ask forgiveness of those who have been
      harmed;
to give forgiveness to those who have harmed.

May God be glorified once again in our midst.

CONFESSION OF RESPONSIBILITY

Representatives of each group come forward and publicly confess
responsibility for their part in the division, apologize even where
the division was itself not intended or desired, and express determination never again to contribute to such destructiveness.

SIGN OF RECONCILIATION

Presider: Before God and before this assembly
you have acknowledged your sin

and have recognized the sinful results
of your own best intentions.
Your thoughts, words, and deeds
have caused division in our world.
From now on you shall bring peace.
I invite you all to turn to those
who were once so distant from you,
and to greet them now in the peace of Christ.

The greeting of peace is now shared among the members of the groups.

COMMUNAL ABSOLUTION

Presider: We turn from the Lord, when we turn from each
            other.
            We turn back to the Lord, when we greet each
            other in peace.

            (with hands extended)

            The Lord God has created you
            to be brother and sister upon the earth,
            to care for one another
            and to be agents of peace.

            May God continue to create you anew.
            May you find God's own loving heart within
            you.

All: Amen.

Presider: Our Lord Jesus Christ
            has called you his friends
            and enlisted you in his work
            of reconciling all people.

            May Christ deepen the reconciliation
            that is yours this day
            and fill you with his peace.

All: Amen.

Presider: The Holy Spirit, Spirit of Love
            has softened the hardness of your hearts
            and opened your lives
            to God's own pardon and peace.

> May this same Spirit breathe life into you
> and make you true givers of life
> to all whom you meet.

All: Amen.

Presider: And I absolve you all from your sins
in the name of the Father +, and of the Son,
and of the Holy Spirit.

All: Amen.

Concluding Rite

Presider: Let us pray together as the Lord Jesus Christ
has taught us to pray:

All: Our Father . . . . But deliver us from evil.
For the kingdom . . . forever and ever. Amen.

Presider: Let us give thanks and praise to God.

All: Glory to God in the highest,
and peace to his people on earth . . . .

In silence, the representatives of the two groups come forward, each with a lighted candle in hand, and together light the single, larger candle that stands in the midst of the assembly. They then extinguish their own candles and place them aside.

The liturgy may conclude with a joyous song.

Commentary: Content

The rituals themselves are fairly self-explanatory. Suffice it to say that the first part is modeled after the installation to ministries and the second after a service of communal reconciliation and forgiveness. A service of this kind is truly the proper setting for communal absolution, at the end of a long process where forgiveness and reconciliation have been achieved.

The second part of this suggested ritual may well be adaptable for yet another reconciliation situation which is hinted at, but nowhere directly addressed in this volume. That situation is the alienation of a *group toward an individual*. People fall through the "cracks" in institutions. People can be radically harmed by institutions. It would be nice to imagine a way in which institutions can acknowledge such responsibility, and seek forgiveness of the individual so harmed. That may be a variant on the ritual presented here which this ritual helps to inspire.

Commentary: Principles

In the closing section of the historical essay presented in this volume, four kinds of action of the larger Church were noted as actions that might help in the ongoing process of reconciling groups: prophecy, conciliar action, mediation, and interdict. The last is in fact not helpful because of its reliance on power, a reliance which too forcefully adapts the "over-against" stance. Such pressure is diametrically opposed to the dynamic of service which the reconciliation of groups demands. The model of council and synod is a bit grand, but if properly scaled down, it does name the dynamic of deliberation that is absolutely necessary if reconciliation is to be advanced among groups. If they do not talk, they cannot be reconciled. Prophecy and mediation are helpful, but they must be broadened beyond any mere reference to Church structures, just as reconciliation itself needs to be broadened beyond the liturgical act.

Reconciliation is a human process which is involved and long. Sometimes a formal reconciliation act can occur as something which the groups flow into naturally or are helped to by the prophet or mediator. Many times, however, it cannot. The primary concern, it must be recalled again, is not with a ritual but with the full scope of the reconciling ministry, and it must be a total ministry of "being with."

The rituals suggested here are not sufficient to achieve reconciliation. They may not even be necessary. While they are offered here in some detail, it must be kept in mind that they can only be suggestions of what might be of service should the process indicate their value. While they are offered here in full Christian sacramental garb, they may, if useful, have to be radically adapted to more general religious or even simply human tones. They are an attempt to respond to the challenge posed by the reconciliation of groups and the fundamental faith of the Christian Church that in Christ all division is overcome. Most important, in whatever guise or garb, the truth they express must somehow enter the fabric of human life.

Final Remark and Challenge

An imaginative work should end with a challenge to the imagination. Let this be it. It is clear that the task of reconciliation is not exhausted by the examples set forth in this volume. Forgiveness is called for wherever sin produces a harmful effect. Reconciliation is needed wherever division and alienation shows its ugly head. Set your imagination to work. How, for example, could this fourth ritual be tailored for the reconciliation of a group with an individual it has harmed? How might a ritual such as the first alternative serve to initiate youngsters into the praxis of reconciliation? And beyond the rituals presented here, in what other ways can the reconciliation of Christ be enfleshed in life and captured in ritual form? It is a task for the imagination. Just imagine!

Index

Abba
  as conscience, 53-56
  as source of wholeness and peace, 54
Adolescence in Erikson's psychosocial stages, 23
Adulthood in Erikson's psychosocial stages, 23
Alienation-withdrawal, 49
American ideas, 18
Anamnesis of Jesus, 56
Aquinas, St. Thomas, 69, 124
Atonement, Christian Day of, 131
Autonomy, 24

Baptism, as initial act of forgiveness of sin, 76-77
Barry, William, 65
Bernardin, Joseph Cardinal, 16
Bernstein, Leonard, 12
Blondell, Robert, 16

Canonical penance, 14, 79-80
Canons on sacrament of penance, 83
Capps, Donald, 24
Chalon, Synod of, 123
Christian Day of Atonement. See Atonement, Christian Day of
Church, as sacrament of reconciliation, 13; mission of, 14
Collins, Mary, O.S.B., 16
Common denominator in reconciling groups, 149, 151
Community, 104-5
Conciliar action, in reconciling process, 88, 164
Conflict, developmental, 24

Conscience
  description of, 51-53
  early development of, 25
  formation of, 47
  and three levels of division, 55
  as voice of Abba, 55
Consent and refusal, 62-63
Constitution on the Sacred Liturgy, 104, 123-24
Control, 24-25
Conversion and transformation, 59-68
Council of Trent, 83
Countercultural experience, 40-42
Cuenin, Walter, 112
Cultural forces of division. See Division in American culture
Culture
  as factor in reconciliation, 19
  influence on reconciliation, 18
  as source of group conflict, 39
Curran, Charles E., 68

Death and sin, parallels of, 65
Didache, 78, 79
Distributive divisions of groups. See Divisions, distributive
Divisions
  alternatives to, 19
  examples of intrapersonal, 45
  interpersonal, 48-50
  moral-religious, level of, 47
Division in American culture, 18-19
Divisions
  distributive, 34, 147, 149
  ideological, 34-35, 147, 149

levels of, 45–48
structural, 147, 149
Divisions of groups, kinds of, 33–36

Early childhood in Erikson's
    psychosocial stages, 23
"Economic" model of penance, 81–82
Edinger, E.F., 20, 21, 22
Ego, in Erikson's theories, 24
Ego boundaries, 27
Environment, role of in human
    development, 24
Erikson, Erik H., 22–26
Eucharist, as sacrament of
    reconciliation, 56, 76–78
Eucharistic act, goal of, 57
Evil, 143–45
Exorcism, 129

Fall of humanity, myth of, 21
Females, early psychological
    development of, 26–28
Festival of Reconciliation, 16
Forgiveness, sacrament of, 13
Freedom, Ricoeur theory of, 62

Gallagher, J. F., 72
Gender identity, 26–28, 29
Global sin, 14
Gregory of Nazianzus, 52
Group reconciliation
    difficulties of, 40-42
    ministry of, 148-51
Groups
    distributive divisions of, 34
    ideological divisions of, 34–35
    structural divisions of, 35–36
Groups in conflict, 33–36
Growing up in American culture, 19
Guilt, absence of, 38–39

Handwashing in reconciliation ritual,
    143
Healing, sacramental, 68
Hoeffner, Robert, 72
Hope, 59–60

Ideological divisions of groups. See
    Divisions, ideological
Ignatius, Spiritual Exercises of, 64–65
Images, negative and positive, 50
Individualism in American culture,
    18
Individuation, and reconciliation,
    22
    definition of, 21
Indulgences, 82
Infancy in Erikson's Psychosocial
    Stages, 23
Institutional-religious level of
    division. See Divisions, levels of
Interdict, and reconciliation, 88, 164
Interpersonal division. See Division,
    interpersonal
Irish penitentials, 81

Jesus as Word of God, 51–56
Jewish Day of Atonement, 131
Jung, Carl, 20–22

Kairos, 149, 150
Kübler-Ross, Elisabeth, 65

Laity, ministry of in reconciliation
    rite, 110–11
"Law court" model of sacrament of
    penance, 83
Liminality in passage rite, 66–67
Liturgical enactment of
    reconciliation, 13
Liturgical rites, new, 84–87
Loftus, John A., 71
Lynch, William, 59–62, 65

Macmurray, John, 49, 149
Males, early psychological
    development of, 26–28
Mature Adulthood in Erikson's
    Psychosocial Stages, 23
Mediation as means to reconciliation,
    88, 164
Metz, Johannes, 53
Ministry of reconciliation of groups,
    process of, 148

Mission of Church. *See* Church, mission of

Moral-religious level of division. *See* Division, levels of

Needs, in reconciliation rites, 85–86

Negative aspects of being an individual, 21

Negative images in reconciliation. *See* Images, negative and positive

Ordained, liturgical ministry of, 125

Ordo Poenitentiae, 84

Original sin, 21

Origins of sacraments, Latin conception of, 74

Passage, three stages of, 66

Paternalistic system, 35

Peace movement, 19

Personal sin. *See* Sin, personal

Play Age in Erikson's Psychosocial Stages, 23

Poetry, as means to humble and heal, 63

Positive aspects of being an individual, 21

Positive images in reconciliation. *See* Images, negative and positive

Presence, ministry of, 148

Presider, as minister of prayer, 124

Private penance, 14, 81–83

Prophecy in reconciling process, 87, 164

Psychological challenges toward reconciliation, 20

Psychological development, early, 26–28

Psychosocial Stages of Development, 22–23

Reaggregation in passage rite, 66–67

Reconciliation
in the Eucharist, 58
as gift of God, 43
goal of, 13

infrequency of use of sacrament, 93

as mission of the Church, 43

origins of sacrament of, 74–77

Rites I, II, III, (official), 84, 85, 86, 94, 95

sacrament of, 13, 59, 73, 127, 152

Reconciliation and forgiveness, 43, 44

Reconciliation of group conflicts, 37

Reconciliation of groups
difficulties of, 41-42
and sacrament of penance, 39-40

Reconciliation rite, need for, 94

Reconciliation rituals of post-Vatican II, 84–87, 94–95

Refusal and consent, 62–63

Responsibility, and guilt, 39
emphasis in group reconciliation ritual, 151

Restitution, 48–49

Ricoeur, Paul, 62–64, 65

Rites of Reconciliation (official). *See* Reconciliation, Rites I, II, III

Ritual
functions of, 150-51
liturgical, 71
role in conversion and transformation, 64-69
as service, 150
value of, 151

Roman Rite for Reconciliation of Individual Penitents, 122

Roy, Paul, 45, 46, 75, 76, 80, 81, 111

Rubin, Lillian, 26–28

Sacramental effectiveness, 69

Sacramental reconciliation of groups. *See* Reconciliation of groups

Sacrament of reconciliation. *See* Reconciliation, sacrament of

School Age in Erikson's Psychosocial Stages, 23

Second Vatican Council. *See* Vatican Council II

Self, Carl Jung theory of, 20

Self-control, 25

Separation in American culture. *See* Division in American culture

Sin, 13, 14, 16, 46–48, 68
  confession of in healing process, 64
  and death, parallels of, 65
  new understanding of, 103
  personal, 14, 48, 127, 130–31
  social, 128, 130, 144

Social sin, as destructive reality, *See* Sin, social

Spirit of God and reconciliation, 75–76

Spiritual Exercises of St. Ignatius. *See* Ignatius, Spiritual Exercises of

Structural divisions of groups. *See* Divisions, structural

Surviving in American culture, 19

Symbols, power of, 103–4

Table prayers, 143

Timing, in reconciliation of groups, 149

Toledo, Third Synod of, 123

Transcendence, 62–63

Transformation
  inner, 87

  process of, 59-68
  spirit of, 75

Trent, Council of, 83

Trust, 30, 54–55

Uniqueness, value of, 18

Values, cultural, 18–19

Vatican Council II, 16, 83, 86

Vietnam veterans, 36

Women
  infants' early identification with, 27
  need for in reconciliation ministry, 111

Women's movement, 19

Woods, Denis, 74, 86, 87

Word, integral to sacrament of penance, 58

Word of God, enacted in sacrament, 51

World Council of Churches, 88

Young Adulthood in Erikson's Psychosocial Stages, 23